my revisi⏻n notes

Rewarding Learning

CCEA GCSE
ICT

D1494641

Siobhan Matthewson

Gerry Lynch

Margaret Debbadi

HODDER
EDUCATION

The Publishers would like to thank the following for permission to reproduce copyright material:

Photo credits

p.11 Getty Images/Fuse; **p.25** *TL* by-studio – Fotolia, *TM* Thanh lam – Fotolia, *TR* Feng Yu – Fotolia, *BM* © iStockphoto.com/Karl Yamashita, *B* Xuejun li – Fotolia; **p.26** *all* Aniuszka – Fotolia, **p.30** *T* OmegaTransFer – Fotolia, *B* weissdesign – Fotolia; **p.36** *T* Hugh Threlfall/Alamy, *B* Judith Collins / Alamy; **p.49** *T* Ewa Walicka – Fotolia, *B* Getty Images/Tetra images RF; **p.50** *T* Krzysiek z Poczty – Fotolia, *BL* Justin Maresch - Fotolia *BR* Vidady – Fotolia; **p.51** *T* liquidImage – Fotolia, *M* David J. Green / Alamy, *B* Konstantin Shevtsov – Fotolia; **p.52** *T* ussatlantis – Fotolia, *M* © iStockphoto.com/Mike McCune, *B* © yuka26 - Fotolia.com; **p.53** *T* © Ragnarock/shutterstock, *B* Ilja Maölk – Fotolia; **p.54** *T* Yong Hian Lim – Fotolia, *B* Rafa Irusta – Fotolia; **p.58** Feng Yu – Fotolia; **p.60** Kurt De Bruyn – Fotolia, **p.64** *L* © amana images inc./Alamy, *R* cphoto – Fotolia; **p.83** *T* ZHANG YUWEI/LANDOV/Press Association Images, *B* Bernhard Classen / Alamy; **p.88** *T* Vladislav Gajic – Fotolia, *B* Rui Vieira/PA Archive/Press Association Images.

Orders: please contact Bookpoint Ltd, 130 Milton Park, Abingdon, Oxon OX14 4SB. Telephone: (44) 01235 827720. Fax: (44) 01235 400454. Lines are open 9.00 – 5.00, Monday to Saturday, with a 24-hour message answering service. Visit our website at www.hoddereducation.co.uk

© Siobhan Matthewson, Gerry Lynch and Margaret Debbadi
First published in 2011 by
Hodder Education,
An Hachette UK Company
338 Euston Road
London NW1 3BH

Impression number   5
Year   2015   2014

Cover photo Kayros Studio – Fotolia
Typeset in 12pt Cronos Pro Light by Phoenix Photosetting, Chatham, Kent ME4 4TZ
Printed in Spain

A catalogue record for this title is available from the British Library

ISBN: 978 1444 147568

Get the most from this book

This book will help you revise Units 1, 2 and 3 of the new CCEA ICT GCSE specification. You can use the contents list on pages 2 and 3 to plan your revision, topic by topic. Tick each box when you have:

1 revised and understood a topic

2 tested yourself

3 checked your answers online

You can also keep track of your revision by ticking off each topic heading through the book. You may find it helpful to add your own notes as you work through each topic.

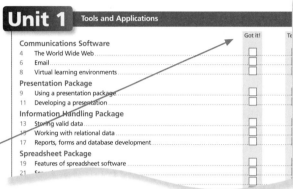

Tick to track your progress

Exam tip

Throughout the book there are exam tips that explain how you can boost your final grade.

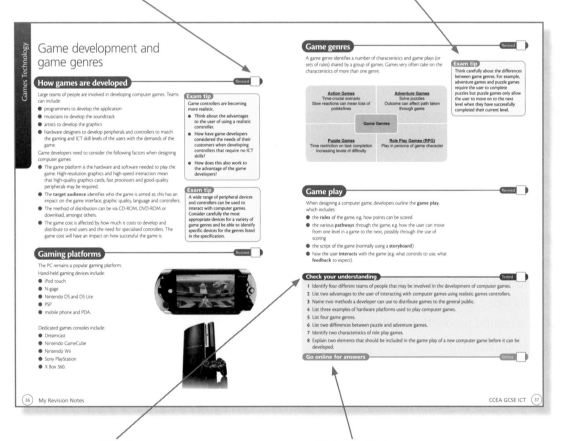

Check your understanding

Use these questions at the end of each section to make sure that you have understood every topic.

Go online

Go online to check your answers at www.therevisionbutton.co.uk/myrevisionnotes.

Contents and revision planner

When you have worked through each section, you will understand these topics. Tick them off as you work through the units.

Unit 1 — Tools and Applications

Unit 2 — Multimedia and Games Technology

Unit 3 — Understanding ICT Systems in Everyday Life

Answers to Check your understanding – online at
www.therevisionbutton.co.uk/myrevisionnotes

The World Wide Web

What is a search engine?

- A search engine allows a user to enter keywords or phrases to locate relevant websites.
- A search engine has access to a large database of websites.
- Google is an example of a common search engine.
- Search engines include an advanced search facility for more experienced users.

Searching techniques

It is important to employ a variety of techniques when using a search engine.

Technique	Description
Use capital and small letters	If you enter keywords and phrases in small (lower case) letters into the search engine, it returns websites that contain the words in either lower or upper case.
Use wildcards	The asterisk (*) represents any character in a keyword; for example, enter colo*r to return websites containing either 'color' or 'colour'.
Use quotation marks	If you put quotation marks (" ") around keywords or phrases, the websites returned must contain that exact phrase.
Put keywords in order of importance	If you enter the most important keywords first, the results will be better.
Use plus (+) and minus (-)	The plus sign in front of a keyword means that the websites must contain it. The minus sign in front of a keyword means that the websites must *not* contain it.
Use complex logic	Complex logic involves using AND, OR and NOT in the search criteria: ● *school AND pupil* returns websites that contain both 'school' and 'pupil'. ● *school OR pupil* returns websites that contain either 'school' or 'pupil'. ● *school NOT pupil* returns websites that contain 'school' but not 'pupil'.

Exam tip

When setting up a search, follow these guidelines:

1 Make a plan.
2 Build a simple initial search, usually one or two keywords.
3 Test the initial search.
4 Add one refinement at a time to the working search and perform it.

What is a website address?

Every website has a unique address. The website address is also known as a Uniform Resource Locator (URL). It is made up of a protocol, a domain name, a top level domain (TLD) and a country code.

Exam tip

Learn the different parts of a web address.

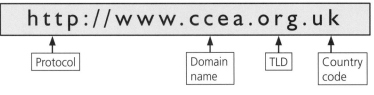

http://www.ccea.org.uk

Protocol — Domain name — TLD — Country code

What is a web browser?

Revised

Browsers are software programs that allow you to access information on websites. Surfing the web is made possible by web browsers. Microsoft Internet Explorer is an example of a web browser. Web browsers have common features that include those shown in the table.

Feature	Description
Back · Forward	These buttons enable the user to visit the previous or next page visited.
Refresh	This button enables the user to update the webpage to take account of any changes that have occurred since the page was downloaded.
Home	This button enables the user to return to their home page.
Search	This button enables the user to search a webpage using keywords.
Favorites	This button enables the user to store addresses of websites that they access frequently.
History	This button enables the user to see websites that have been accessed over a specific timescale (days or weeks), set by the user.
Print	This button enables the user to print the current webpage.
Edit	This button launches a common piece of software, such as a wordprocessor, database or spreadsheet, to allow the user to edit the contents of the information.

Exam tip

Be able to state four features of a typical web browser.

Check your understanding

Tested

1 Complete the table with the name that matches the description.

What am I?	Description
	Allows you to access information on websites
	Allows you to enter keywords or phrases to locate relevant websites
	A Uniform Resource Locator (URL)

2 State three features of a typical web browser.

Go online for answers

Online

Email

- The **inbox** displays all emails that have been sent to you. They can be arranged by date, alphabetical order, size, etc.

- The **date and time** are automatically shown on each email, allowing you to view emails by date sent, or even by the time sent on a given day.

- The **To**, **Cc** and **Bcc** boxes allow you to enter the relevant email addresses.

- The **Subject** box allows you to enter a title for your message.

- The textbox allows you to enter the message.

- The **Address Book** button allows you access to your electronic address book where you can store and access all your contacts' email addresses.

- The **Signature** button allows you to save your personal details for automatic inclusion in emails being created.

You can create **distribution lists** of contacts for the purpose of sending group emails.

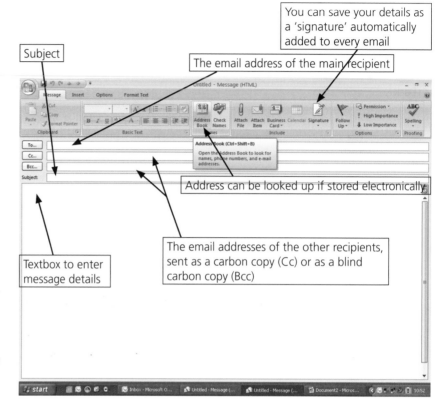

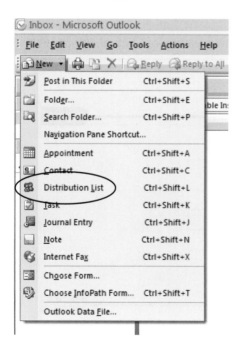

The **Attachment** button allows you to send copies of files (e.g. text, graphics, sound clips or video clips) with your email.

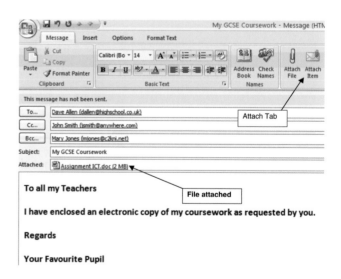

Use the **Send** button to send the message. If you have received a message you can also **Reply**, **Forward** it to another person's email address or **Delete** it.

Message options allow you to:

● allocate a **priority** (importance) to a message
● track an email by requesting delivery and read receipts
● specify a date and time for delivery of the message.

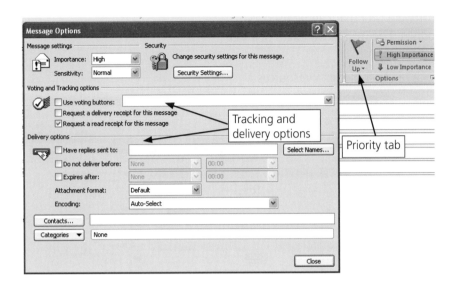

You can create personal folders to store emails from the same contact together.

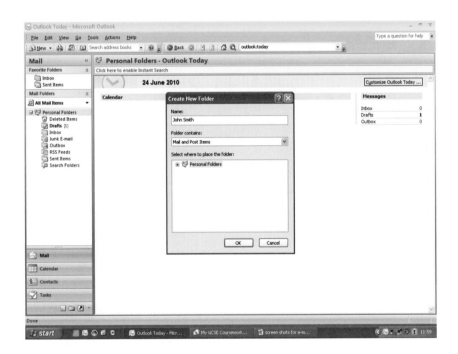

Check your understanding

Tested

1 Distinguish between a Cc and a Bcc email address.
2 You want to send your teacher an email including a word-processed essay. Outline the steps you would take.
3 Apart from the Address Book, state three other features of an email program.

Go online for answers

Online

Virtual learning environments

A virtual learning environment (VLE) is a software tool that can be used in a school to assist in the delivery of online courses. The main advantages of a VLE are:

- an organised central storage method for a number of digital resources
- shared resources for teaching and learning
- access to multimedia that appeals to different learning styles
- learning beyond the classroom with 24/7 access available to individuals
- personalised learning – lessons tailored to individual pupil requirements.

LearningNI is an example of a VLE. It allows a student to:

- access courses on which they are currently enrolled
- create a personal web page
- access a library of electronic resources
- receive announcements
- access emails and other services.

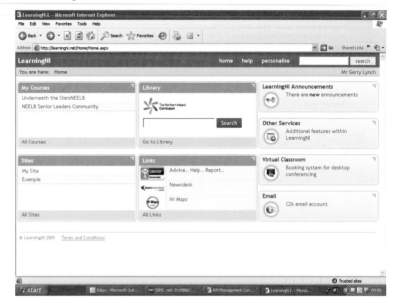

Other services available to learners on a VLE include:

- the ability to upload files
- access to a personal timetable
- participation in online discussion forums.

Services available to teachers on a VLE include:

- tools for administration
- reporting on pupil progress
- tracking tools that allow teachers to monitor the progress of pupils who are taking part in and being assessed on VLE courses.

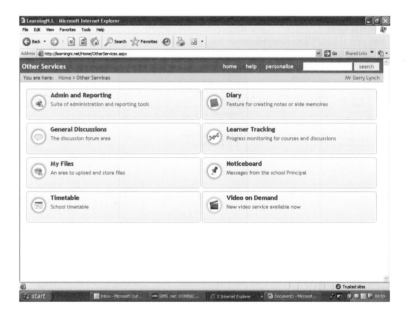

> **Exam tip**
>
> Be able to state three advantages of a typical VLE.

1 State three advantages of using a VLE in teaching and learning.
2 State three services available to a student who is using a VLE.

Go online for answers   Online

Using a presentation package

The features of a presentation package

A presentation package combines text, graphics, sound and video. It can also be called multimedia.

● **Text** can be formatted using the font options provided by the package.

● **Animation** features allow users to:

■ add moving images

■ create a path for objects when they enter or leave a slide

■ add effects (for example, 'fly in') to objects when they enter or leave the slide.

● Predefined **slide layouts** and **templates** help users to develop professional presentations quickly.

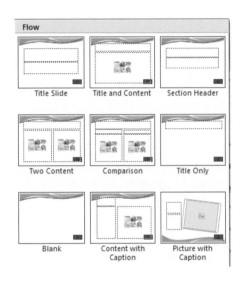

● **Headers** and **footers** can include the date and slide number.

● **Slide notes** enable the developer to include details that can be read or referred to when presenting the information.

● **Backgrounds** and **themes** change the text colours and background graphics on the slide.

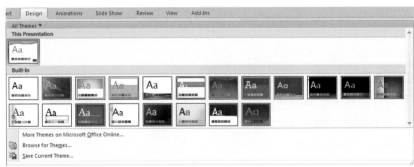

● **Navigation buttons** and **hyperlinks** allow users to select different pathways through the presentation. The user clicks on a link or button to move from one slide to another.

Exam tip

Navigation buttons and hyperlinks structure the way in which users can view the presentation. They allow users to go to different slides. They can change the sequence in which the slides are viewed.

● **Master slides** contain items that appear on every slide. In the example, every slide has a Home button that returns the user to the first slide and a footer.

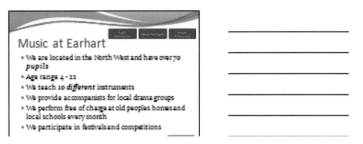

● You can **print** slides in a variety of layouts for different uses. Handout layout shows three slides per page with a set of lines beside each slide for writing.

● A **slide transition** determines how the slide appears on the screen (for example, it may 'dissolve' or 'fly in'). You can vary some aspects of the transition:

  ■ A **transition sound** plays as the slide enters the screen.

  ■ The **transition speed** determines how quickly or slowly the slide arrives onto the screen.

  ■ The **timings** and **advance slide** options can play the presentation automatically or loop it.

● You can set timings for individual slides so that they appear on screen after a set number of seconds.

● You can **link** or **embed** objects, such as graphs, tables and sounds, from other software packages.

Check your understanding
Tested

1 Which of the following are features of a presentation package?
  a) performing calculations
  b) recording data
  c) including multimedia
  d) formatting text.

2 What is the function of navigation buttons in presentation software?

3 What is the function of a master slide in a presentation?

4 List the features of presentation software that allow the display sequence of the presentation to change.

5 What is the difference between linking and embedding an object?

Go online for answers
Online

Developing a presentation

Planning is an important part of developing a presentation. Before using the software it is important that you consider the content and structure of your presentation:

- Define the purpose of the presentation.
- Identify the **target audience** and any special requirements it might have.
- Produce a **storyboard** (a plan for the layout and content of each slide within the presentation); a storyboard will also help you decide how slides link together.
- Collect the digital assets (the pictures, sounds, videos and other files that you intend to include in the presentation).

> **Exam tip**
>
> The target audience is the group of people who you will give the presentation to or who will view the presentation. Your presentation should take account of the needs of the target audience. For example, young children have different requirements from adults.

The figure shows a basic plan for a presentation that will include seven slides. It is easy to see how the slides link together and the title for each slide. It shows *the structure* of the presentation.

The next stage would be to develop a more detailed storyboard that shows the text or digital assets which appear on each slide.

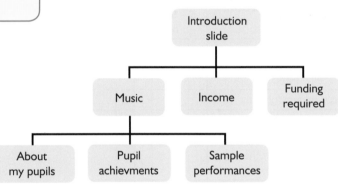

Testing a presentation Revised

Before using a presentation with the target audience, you should test it:

- to ensure that there are no grammar or spelling mistakes
- to ensure that all pictures are present
- to ensure that all hyperlinks and buttons link to the correct slides
- to ensure that any embedded or linked files operate as expected
- to ensure that any special effects work as planned
- to rehearse any timings set.

A good way of testing a presentation is to allow someone else to view it. Give the person who will test the presentation a checklist such as the following:

- For each slide within the presentation:
  - Read the text and ensure it is accurate and correct (perform a spell check).

- Check that the hyperlinks and the buttons on the slide go to the correct location or slide.
- Check that all pictures are present.
- Play all videos or sound files and ensure they work appropriately.
- Check that special effects (such as timings) do not overlap or affect other events on the slide.
● Check that all slides on the storyboard exist in the presentation.

Evaluating a presentation
Revised

If you have completed Unit 1, you will have evaluated your presentation.

You evaluate a presentation to:

● comment on ease of navigation
● ensure that it is suitable for the target audience
● consider how well it communicates the message
● consider how well it makes use of digital and multimedia assets
● identify strengths and weaknesses in the presentation
● identify areas for improvement in the presentation.

You can use a table such as this one to evaluate a presentation.

My presentation:	1 – Strongly disagree 5 – Strongly agree					Evidence to support my statements	Areas for improvements
	1	2	3	4	5		
Is fully tested							
Is working correctly							
Is suitable for the intended audience							
Communicates the message well							
Makes appropriate use of multimedia assets							

Exam tips

It is good to:
● plan effectively
● take account of the target audience
● test fully
● make appropriate use of presentation features
● evaluate the finished product.

Beware of:
● over-using animation and special effects so that they hamper the real message getting across
● adding too much text to a slide (a viewer can only read a small amount if someone is talking to them at the same time).

Check your understanding
Tested

1 What actions would you undertake when planning a presentation?
2 What are 'digital assets'?
3 What is meant by the words 'target audience'?
4 Why is it important to test a presentation?
5 What aspects of a presentation should be tested?
6 Why is it important to evaluate a presentation?
7 What advice would you give to a student who is about to create a presentation for a group of school children?

Go online for answers
Online

Storing valid data

Structuring data

An information handling package is designed to allow users to **collect** and **structure** data. Data is structured into **records** and **fields**.

Fields

Each field has a **data type**, for example:

- **Numeric** – data takes on a numeric value and can be used in calculations.
- **Text** – data can be made up of letters or letters and numbers.
- **Date** – data takes on a value which is formatted as a date.
- **Boolean** – data can take only two values, normally yes and no.

> **Exam tip**
>
> There are several data types. You should be able to name each data type and suggest appropriate data types for different fields.

Pupil	
Field Name	Data Type
PupilNumber	Number
Surname	Text
Forename	Text
Street	Text
Town	Text
Postcode	Text
AccompanistRequired	Yes/No
DateJoined	Date/Time

Tables

Tables are made up of **records** and each record is made up of a set of **fields**. In a file or table, a row usually represents a record and a set of field values are contained in a column.

The figure shows a table structure set up in a database package. The table is called Pupil.

Records

A record is a unit of data that is made up of a number of **fields**. There is one record per item in a database table. Here is a typical record from the Pupil table.

PupilNumber	Surname	Forename	Street	Town	Postcode	AccompanistRequired	DateJoined
1000	Black	Ellen	23 Long Road	Coleraine	BT99 0JJ	Yes	12-Dec-03

Key field

A relational database allows the user to set a **key field** for each table. The key field is a value that *uniquely identifies* a record in the table. The key field for the Pupil table is PupilNumber, as shown by the key symbol beside the PupilNumber field.

> **Exam tip**
>
> A key field is also called a 'primary key'.

Pupil		
Field Name	Data Type	Description
PupilNumber	Number	Pupil Number - Primary (or Key) Field
Surname	Text	Name of pupil
Forename	Text	
Street	Text	
Town	Text	
Postcode	Text	
AccompanistRequired	Yes/No	
DateJoined	Date/Time	

Formatting fields

A way of controlling the way in which data is to be held in a database is to use some of the data formatting tools when designing a table. For example:

- A date can be stored in a number of formats, e.g. Medium Date 24-May-11 or Short Date 24/05/11.
- An **input mask** defines the format of the data being entered.

Microsoft Access has some readymade input masks available, for example, for a postcode. When developing a solution you can create your own input masks (such as those shown in the table). A field with an input mask can only accept data in this format.

Input mask	Acceptable values
(000) 00-00000	(028) 71-77775
(0000) AAA-AAAAA	(9445) 555-PUPIL
#999	-20 123
LL00 0LL	EC12 8XZ (a postcode)

Validating data

Revised

Validation ensures that data is:

- present
- in the correct range
- in the correct format.

Most database packages provide a feature that allows you to enter validation rules for data. You can include different validation checks before data is entered into a table.

The Data and Information section of Unit 3 gives details about the ways in which data can be validated when it is being input to a computer system.

The validation rule shown is for the PupilNumber field. It must be in the range 1000–1100. If the data entered is outside this range (in this case, a PupilNumber of 12001), an **error message** appears.

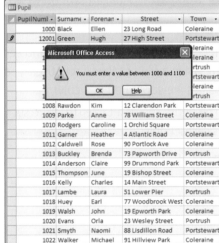

> **Exam tip**
>
> Remember the following validation checks:
>
> - presence check
> - length check
> - type check
> - range check
> - format check.

Check your understanding

Tested

1 How is a table made up in a database?

2 List four data types.

3 What data types would you recommend to store:
   a) a date of birth
   b) a surname
   c) a gender?

4 What is the purpose of validation?

5 List four types of validation check.

6 What is the function of a key field in a database?

Go online for answers

Online

Working with relational data

Creating relationships

A **relationship** is a *link between two tables*. The links are made using a common field (a field that is contained in both tables).

The advantage of linking or relating tables is that:

● it can reduce the amount of data which has to be stored

● it makes the searching and sorting of data more efficient.

One pupil can take many grade examinations (and get many receipts). The relationship is known as a **one-to-many** relationship. The PupilNumber field occurs in both tables and the tables are linked on it. Ellen Black is taking three grade examinations and you can see her data in the two tables.

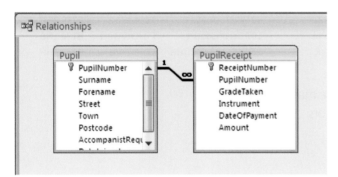

Using a wizard

A **wizard** is software that helps the user to complete a task, step by step. The user clicks buttons and makes selections about data but does not have to know how the wizard works.

An information handling package usually provides wizards for complex tasks, such as creating reports, queries and forms.

Using mail merge

Users can create standard documents and merge records from the database onto the documents. This is called a **mail merge**.

To create a customised letter and send it to many people:

1 Create the standard letter with merge fields.

2 Select the data source – such as a table or query – to provide the records for the mail merge.

3 Select the appropriate merge fields from the data source and include them on the letter.

4 Merge the data from the data source onto the letter.

5 Print the personalised letters.

Selecting, sorting and searching using criteria

A query facility allows users to **search** or **select** records from the database which fit certain **criteria**.

To carry out a query:

1 Select a table.

2 Select fields from the table.

3 Enter the criteria.

4 Run the query.

5 View the results.

For example, to make a list of all the pupils who require an accompanist, the criteria would be set to AccompanistRequired to Yes.

The results of a query are shown in table format. Note that the results of the query are sorted in ascending order of surname (as specified in the query).

Surname	Forename	Street	Town	Postcode
Barkley	Susan	12 Culmore Ave	Portrush	BT95 5TT
Black	Ellen	23 Long Road	Coleraine	BT99 0JJ
Buckley	Brenda	73 Papworth Drive	Portrush	BT95 5HG
Caldwell	Rose	90 Portlock Ave	Coleraine	BT99 3GH
Cunningham	John	107 Baronscourt	Portstewart	BT96 1NB
Doherty	Jack	16 Greenpark Close	Coleraine	BT99 7HH

If you just type a value into a criterion, the value in the table must match it (the condition is =). You can use other conditional operators:

● < (less than)

● <= (less than or equal to)

● > (greater than)

● >= (greater than or equal to).

For example, to find everyone who has joined since 2009, the condition is DateJoined >= 01/01/2010.

Criteria can be combined using logical operators, such as **AND**, **OR** and **NOT**.

Operator	Meaning	Sample criteria using two criteria
AND	If all criteria are fulfilled, the record is included in the results.	Flute players who require an accompanist: AccompanistRequired=Yes AND Instrument=Flute
OR	If any one or more of the criteria are fulfilled, the record is included in the results.	All people who play flute or violin: Instrument=Flute OR Instrument=Violin
NOT	Only records that do not fulfil the criteria are included in the results.	All pupils who require an accompanist excluding violin players: AccompanistRequired=Yes AND Instrument=NOT Violin

A query can be carried out on data in two tables at the same time as long as the tables are related.

Check your understanding

1 What is a relationship in a database?

2 What is the advantage of linking tables?

3 List four steps necessary to complete a mail merge.

4 What is a wizard?

5 List three wizards available in database software.

6 What is the purpose of a query in a database?

7 How can a query be created in a database?

8 How can criteria be combined in a database?

9 List three logical operators and their meaning.

Go online for answers

Online

Reports, forms and database development

Creating and formatting reports

Reports can be created using the data in tables or the results of a query. A report is designed for printing but can also be viewed on screen.

Data in reports can be **grouped** and **sorted**.

The figure shows a section of a report that gives information about the grade examinations taken by each pupil. The data has been *grouped by PupilNumber* and *sorted by ReceiptNumber*. The report also calculates the total amount owed by each student.

Pupil Bill Details

PupilNumber	Surname	Forename	ReceiptNumber	GradeTaken	Instrument	DateOfPayment	Amount
1000	Black	Ellen					
			1	Grade 5	Violin	12-Sep-10	£40.00
			5	Grade 5	Piano	15-Sep-10	£30.00
			16	Grade 4	Piano	14-Sep-10	£24.00
							£94.00

It is important that reports produce information which is accurate and complete. The report should be **user friendly** to ensure that the user can make good use of the information.

Using data capture forms

Users can **add, delete** and **update** records using the table view in the database or through a data capture form. Database software provides a method of designing forms for **data capture**.

The figure shows a simple form that allows the user to input data to the Pupil table and the PupilReceipt table.

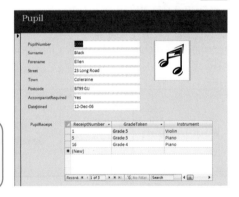

Exam tip

Revise the features of good form design. A well-designed form is **user friendly**. This means it is easy for users to understand and use.

Importing data

A database package has a feature for importing data. Data can be imported from other sources such as a spreadsheet file or a comma-separated-variable (CSV) file. This is useful if data has been created using a different software package.

Importing is generally done using a wizard and the user is taken through the process step by step.

Effective planning

Planning is an important part of developing a database. Before using the software it is important that you consider the user requirements and how you will structure the data to produce the information the user needs:

- List the user requirements in terms of input, processing and output. This will include any reports, queries and forms to be used in the system.
- Identify tasks that the user will need to perform, such as adding, deleting and updating records.
- Identify the data which needs to be collected.

Structuring the data appropriately

- Organise the data into fields, records and tables.
- Select a suitable data type for each field.
- Identify the validation and formatting requirements for each field.
- Identify the key field for each table.
- Identify the relationships that need to be created between tables.
- Identify queries that need to be created to produce output.
- Design data capture forms and reports.

Testing a database solution

Before releasing the database solution to the user, test it to make sure that the user requirements have been met and that there are no errors. When developing a user test for your database or another student's database, consider the following issues:

- Use the list of user requirements developed during planning to ensure that each item on the list has been completed.
- Test the data capture forms to ensure that the data collected is valid and that the forms are user friendly.
- Run queries to ensure that the criteria produce the correct results and that searches are efficient.
- Check reports produced to ensure that they display the correct information in a suitable format.

Evaluating a database solution

Evaluating a database solution involves:

- assessing **fitness for purpose –** how well the database meets the user requirements
- identifying strengths and weaknesses:
  - the **user friendliness** of data capture forms and reports
  - the effectiveness of the searching (queries) and sorting features of your solution
- identifying areas for improvement.

Test the database before you evaluate it as testing will provide some of the answers to these questions. A table such as the one below could be used to help structure your evaluation and testing. This shows one user requirement related to recording pupil details.

Requirement	Met (Yes/No?)	Evidence (Describe which parts of the database show that you have met this requirement.)	Evaluation (How well do you think each part of the database you have described meets the requirements? Give a reason to support your answer.)
Keep a record of her pupils and their details.	Yes	I have created a form called Pupilform. This contains a subform that allows Ruth to enter the data about a pupil and also to enter receipt/payment details. This form works fully and all data is written to the database.	Pupilform is user friendly and clearly explains what is required in each box. I have included a title, but could improve it by adding Ruth's logo.

Check your understanding — Tested

1 What is the purpose of a report in a database? How can the output on a report be organised?

2 What steps should be followed when planning a database solution?

3 How can the data be structured when developing a database solution?

4 How would you test a database solution created by another student?

5 What is the purpose of evaluating a database solution?

Go online for answers — Online

Features of spreadsheet software

Spreadsheet features

Revised

Spreadsheet packages have a number of common features:

● They perform calculations and recalculations automatically.

● They allow results to be displayed in tabular or graphic format.

● They consist of a table divided into rows and columns to produce cells.

● They consist of a number of worksheets.

Cells

All the work in a spreadsheet is carried out by cells:

● Each cell has a column reference (a letter) and a row reference (a number).

● The active cell is clearly highlighted.

● The contents of the active cell are displayed in the data entry bar.

> **Exam tip**
>
> There are several data formats – you should be able to name each format and suggest suitable data types for given cells.

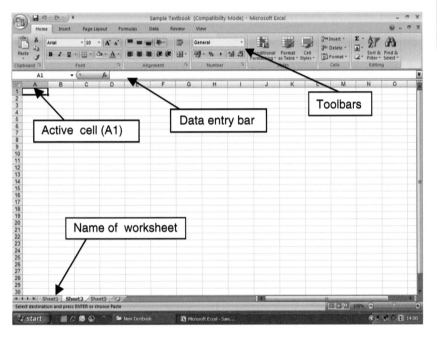

When entering data into a spreadsheet, you can format the data into a specified category.

ABC123 **General** No specific format

12 **Number**

Currency

Accounting

Short Date

Long Date

Time

% **Percentage**

½ **Fraction**

10² **Scientific**

More Number Formats...

● Cells can be further formatted by specifying aspects such as the number of decimal places, font size and style.

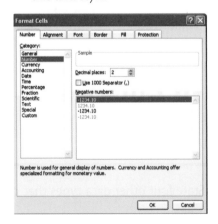

● You can also format the alignment of data in cells.

● To enhance presentation, you can add borders and shading to cells.

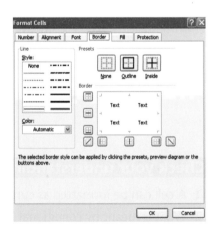

Conditional formatting

Conditional formatting allows you to apply cell shading or font colour to a cell if a specified condition is true.

In this example, values between 91 and 99 will be displayed in red.

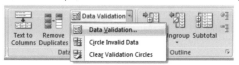

Data validation

Data validation makes it possible to control the values input into a given cell.

In this example, the number represents an assignment mark out of 20. In the Data Validation settings dialogue, you can define the data type (whole number) and a range check to ensure that the values lie between 0 and 20.

You can select the Input Message tab and enter a suitable message to guide the user.

On the Error Alert tab, you can control the style of the error message by selecting Stop, Warning or Information error message.

Check your understanding
Tested

1 A cell can be formatted as currency. State four other data types that could be used when formatting a cell.
2 What is meant by conditional formatting?

Go online for answers
Online

Spreadsheet functions

Revised

SUM function

The SUM function calculates the total of a group of selected cell values.

In the example, =SUM(C5:H5) calculates the total score for all tasks for a pupil. The SUM function automatically updates the value in I5 if any values in the range C5:H5 change.

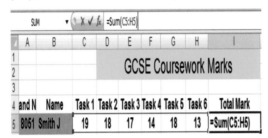

AVERAGE function

The AVERAGE function calculates the average (mean) of a group of selected cell values.

In the example, =AVERAGE(C5:C16) calculates the average score for Task 1. The AVERAGE function automatically updates the value in C19 if any values in the range C5:C16 change.

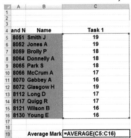

MAX function

The MAX function finds the largest value stored in a group of cells.

For example, =MAX(I5:I16) finds the highest score gained by a single pupil over all the tasks. The MAX function automatically updates the value in C21 if any values in the range I5:I16 change.

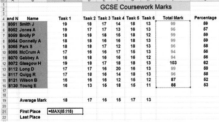

MIN function

The MIN function finds the smallest value stored in a group of cells.

For example, =MIN(I5:I16) finds the lowest score gained by a single pupil over all the tasks. The MIN function automatically updates the value in C22 if any values in the range I5:I16 change.

Other functions and commands

Revised

IF function

The IF function sets the cell value depending on the result of examining a condition: IF the condition is true THEN value 1 ELSE value 2.

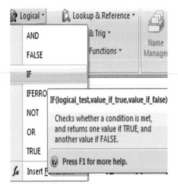

In the example, the teacher wants to give any score greater than 95 the comment 'Excellent' and any score up to 95 a comment 'Well done'. This can be written as:

IF Grand Total > 95 THEN 'Excellent' ELSE 'Well done'

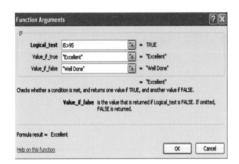

> **Exam tip**
>
> There are several functions available in a spreadsheet – you should be able to name common functions and suggest suitable data functions and data ranges that would be used in given cells.

Fill command

When a function is created, you can easily replicate it across a range of cells.

For example, you can replicate a formula in each cell in the selected column by selecting the Fill menu and the Down option. The Right option on the Fill menu replicates the formula across a row.

The advantage in using this feature is that a formula has only to be entered once. Any relative field references in the formula automatically update to be relevant to the new row or column. For example, as SUM(C5:H5) is copied down, it changes to SUM(C6:H6), SUM(C7:H7) and so on.

If you do not want the cell reference to change when you copy a formula, you can make it an absolute reference. For example, I5 always refers to cell I5 and a formula containing I5 keeps the I5 even if copied down a column or across a row.

Check your understanding

Tested

1 Distinguish between the MAX and MIN functions.
2 Define what is meant by an absolute cell reference.

Go online for answers

Online

Lookup tables and graphs

Lookup tables
Revised

A 'lookup table' provides information to be used elsewhere in the spreadsheet. For example, the teacher has created a table with an index number and a corresponding grade.

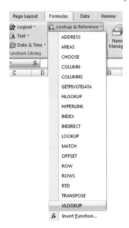

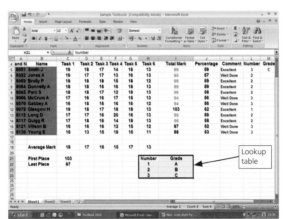

The VLOOKUP function takes the value in a particular cell (e.g. L5) and finds it in the first column of the lookup table (in this case, in cell H24). The function returns the corresponding value in the next column.

In this example, the teacher allocates the number 1, 2 or 3 to each pupil and a grade from the lookup table is automatically placed in the appropriate cell.

Graphs
Revised

- You can decide to present data in graphical form.
- You can select from a list of suitable graphs.
- A wizard guides you through each stage, including selecting:
  - the data value range
  - the labels for each axis
  - the title for the graph
  - other formatting features, such as colour.

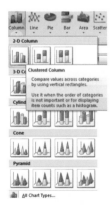

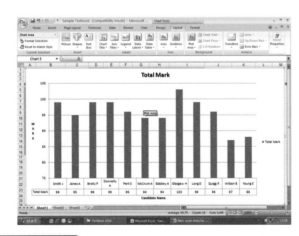

Check your understanding
Tested

1 Describe a VLOOKUP function.
2 State two advantages of using a wizard to produce a graph.

Go online for answers
Online

Testing and evaluating spreadsheets

Revised

Testing a spreadsheet

Before handing over a spreadsheet solution to the client, you should test it to ensure that:

- it meets the user requirements
- the formulas work
- recalculations are automatic when a value in a cell changes
- all data is correctly formatted
- any data validation rules work correctly
- any graphs designed are as expected
- links between worksheets are working.

Evaluating a spreadsheet

Revised

It is also important to evaluate any spreadsheets you create:

- Is the overall appearance of the spreadsheet suitable for the target audience?
- Are labels and text are correctly spelt?
- How well does the spreadsheet make use of fonts, styles and formatting?
- How well does the spreadsheet use data formats and text alignment?
- How well does the spreadsheet use functions and formulas?
- What are the strengths and weaknesses of the spreadsheet?
- How well has the presentation of the results been enhanced using graphs?
- What are the areas for improvement in the spreadsheet?

A table such as the one below could be used to evaluate a spreadsheet.

My spreadsheet:	1 – Strongly disagree 5 – Strongly agree					Evidence to support my statements	Areas for improvements
	1	2	3	4	5		
Is fully tested							
Works correctly, producing accurate results							
Is suitable for user requirements							
Gives clearly presented results, including graphs							
Makes appropriate use of functions and formulas							

It is good to:

✓ plan effectively
✓ take account of all user requirements
✓ test fully after creating a spreadsheet
✓ make appropriate use of spreadsheet features
✓ evaluate the finished product.

Beware of:

✗ using incorrect formulas or functions that lead to errors
✗ using the graph feature if it does not enhance the presentation of results.

Check your understanding

Tested

1 Why is it important to test a spreadsheet?
2 What aspects of a spreadsheet should be tested?
3 Why is it important to evaluate a spreadsheet?
4 What steps can be taken to ensure the results produced on a spreadsheet are accurate?

Go online for answers

Online

Capturing and manipulating graphics

What are graphics?

Revised

Graphics can come in a variety of formats:

- clip art
- **digital** photographs
- word art
- scanned images
- images created using a graphics package
- **animation**.

Devices used to capture graphics

Revised

Graphics that are not created on the computer can be captured using a variety of hardware devices such as:

- a digital camera
- a mobile phone
- a scanner.

Exam tip

Think carefully about other ways these devices can be used to capture images. For example, a digital camera can take a picture of a hard-copy image for import into a computer.

Transferring images from source to software for manipulation

Revised

Graphics not created using a computer must be input into the computer before you can edit them or use them. You can:

- upload them via a cable, e.g. a Universal Serial Bus (USB), that links the device to the computer
- copy them from a memory card (e.g. from a digital camera) using a memory card reader
- transfer them between devices using Bluetooth, infrared or Wi-Fi
- transfer them using flash media, e.g. a USB memory device
- send them via email and then download them on to your computer.

Memory cards are used to provide additional memory in mobile phones, digital cameras, etc.

Exam tip

In an exam, you may be asked to correctly identify the most appropriate hardware for inputting a graphic to a computer. Always consider the original format of the graphic before you answer this question.

Image manipulation tools

Revised

Graphics packages allow users to create and edit digital images:

- Text boxes and text tools can be used to add text to a graphic image (font, text colour, size, etc. can normally be changed).
- Predefined shapes can be selected and drawn.
- Line tools can draw straight, curved or freehand lines.
- Rotate tools allow you to rotate the image around a given point or to a certain angle.
- Stretch handles around a selected image can be used to stretch the image horizontally or vertically.
- Images can be flipped vertically or horizontally.

Text tool

Predefined shapes

Line tool

Rotate tool

Stretch handles

Other image manipulation tools include:

- Zoom – an area of the image can be viewed more closely
- Fill – shapes and areas of an image can be filled with a colour selected from the colour palette

- Crop – an unwanted part of a graphic can be selected and removed from the image

- Grouping – new graphics objects can be created by combining objects; grouped objects can be selected and moved around together.

Exam tip

The examiner may ask you to identify the type of manipulation that has been applied to a graphic by showing you a 'before' and 'after' image.

Check your understanding

Tested

1 Identify three devices that can be used to capture images for import to a computer.
2 Name three different types of graphics.
3 James wants to include a photograph of his new skateboard in a presentation he is doing. Identify two ways James could capture this image for import into his presentation.
4 Explain the difference between the flip and rotate tools in image manipulation software.
5 Identify two other image manipulation tools that are made available in most graphics packages.

Go online for answers

Online

Digital effects and bitmap and vector graphics

Applying effects to digital images
Revised ☐

Many graphics packages allow you to add pre-installed effects to your digital images. Some of these effects include:

● black and white photo

● sepia photo

● oil painting.

Most graphics packages allow you to control the effect using preset formats. With more complex effects, you can control the way they are applied.

Integrating images and text
Revised ☐

A variety of tools are available to assist with the integration of text and images. For example:

● The watermark or washout tool allows text to be read easily over the top of the image.

● The transparency tool allows you remove the colour from a selected portion of an image so the background graphic or text colour is visible.

● The text wrapping tool allows you to determine how the text appears around the graphic.

● The order tool allows you to reorder text and graphics and place items on top of each other.

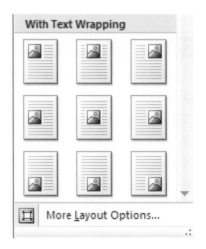

> **Exam tip**
>
> Remember that many of these tools are also available in word-processing and desktop-publishing packages.

Bitmap and vector graphics

Revised

Bitmap graphics:

- store detail about every individual picture element (**pixel**) in the image
- tend to be large files
- can be **compressed** (reduced in size).

The more pixels used to create a bitmap image, the higher the **resolution** of the image is said to be and the better the quality of the image being displayed.

Vector-based graphics:

- store information (e.g. shape, colour and location in the image) about the objects that make up an image
- don't depend on resolution for quality
- can be more easily resized and stretched than bitmap images
- give a much smaller file size than an equivalent bitmap.

> **Exam tip**
>
> If a graphic is compressed it often means a loss in quality of the image represented.

> **Exam tip**
>
> Be able to clearly explain the difference between bitmap and vector graphics. Be ready to compare them in terms of file size, image quality and potential uses.

Impact of image resolution on file size

Revised

- Higher resolution graphics present higher quality images.
- Higher resolution graphics take up more storage space.

This trade-off needs to be considered when selecting the file formats for graphics you are creating for use in webpages, computer games or any other application.

> **Exam tip**
>
> Consider carefully why bitmap images are not suitable for use on webpages. Think about the impact their use would have on the web space used and the time taken to load each image.

Check your understanding

Tested

1 Give two reasons why a bitmap file format is not suitable for storing graphics on a website.
2 Give one reason why graphic designers might prefer to use bitmap graphics.
3 List three characteristics of bitmap graphics.
4 List three characteristics of vector graphics.
5 Explain why there is a trade-off between graphic resolution and file size.
6 Define the term 'resolution'.

Go online for answers

Online

Preparing graphics for a range of uses

Graphic file formats
Revised

Images that have been edited by graphics packages can be saved in a variety of formats.

File type	Description
BMP	Bitmap files hold data about every pixel in the image and tend to be quite large.
GIF	Graphics Interchange Format files are a compressed graphics format. They can be used to represent animated and still graphic images.
JPEG	Joint Photographic Expert Group files are a compressed graphics format. The user can determine the level of compression applied to the image.
PICT	This file format is used for graphics by Apple Macintosh. They are high quality images but they can be compressed.
PNG	Portable Networks Graphics files allow bitmap images to be compressed. They are normally slightly larger than GIF files.
TIFF	Tagged Image File Format stores bitmap images in a format that allows them to be transferred easily between Windows and Apple Macintosh platforms.

Evaluating graphics for use in a website or game
Revised

The file format used depends on what the graphic is to be used for:

● JPEG and GIF file formats are often used for internet-based graphics.

● JPEG is often used for photographs.

● GIF is often used for animated graphic images created using lines and geometric shapes.

● BMP file formats are often used by graphic designers as they can edit graphics at the lowest level (pixel level).

Check your understanding
Tested

1 Identify two suitable file formats for representing graphics on a website.

2 Expand the following acronyms: GIF, TIFF, JPEG, PNG.

3 Identify a suitable file format for representing animated graphics.

4 Give one reason why BMP files are often used by graphic designers.

5 Select the odd one out from this list of file types and give one reason for your answer: BMP, GIF, PNG, TIFF.

6 Apart from representing graphics to be displayed on the internet, identify one appropriate use for the JPEG file format.

Go online for answers
Online

Digital video and sound capture and distribution

Digital video and sound capture

Digital video and digital sound can be captured using a range of devices including: mobile phones, digital cameras and microphones.

- Many **3G** mobile phones and digital cameras include basic facilities for editing digital video files.
- Most devices come with an expansion slot for memory cards to allow for the storage of digital video and sound files.
- Microphones record analogue sound waves that are then converted to digital format.

Exam tip

Consider why the memory card included with most standard mobile phones is not sufficient for the storage of digital video and sound files.

Exam tip

Consider the advantages and disadvantages of being able to record digital video and sound files on portable devices, such as mobile phones.

Exam tip

Think carefully about why sound waves need to be converted to digital format before they can be stored on a mobile phone or computer.

Digital video and sound distribution

Digital video and sound can be distributed to others in a variety of ways:

- **optical storage media** (DVD and CD-ROM)
- internet (email or publishing on websites)
- **Bluetooth**
- **flash technologies**
- **Blu-ray**
- HD-TV.

How you distribute your digital video files affects the file format you use to save them:

- Before you can distribute a digital video or sound file you need to **optimise** it.
- Optimisation means the file is reduced in size so it takes up less web space or storage space.
- Codecs (**compression/decompression** software) are used to carry out the optimisation process.

Exam tips

- You could be asked to select an appropriate method of distributing a digital video or sound file in a given scenario and you may have to give a reason for your answer.
- It is important that you know the characteristics, advantages and disadvantages of each of the media. You should know the storage capacities of each of the storage devices.

Exam tip

Think about how optimisation affects the speed at which a digital video or sound file can be transferred across a network.

Appropriate file formats for web distribution

Revised

Video file formats

File type	Description
.avi	Audio Video Interleave
.fla	Flash Movie Authoring Projects made using Flash can then be saved in Shockwave format (.swf).
.mov	An Apple file format used for storing multimedia files and movies
.mp4	MPEG4 files can be downloaded from the internet for use on portable media players.
.mpeg	Moving Pictures Expert Group
.wmv	Windows Media Video

Exam tip

You may be asked in the examination to identify a variety of file types from given file extensions or acronyms.

Sound file formats

File type	Description
AIF	Audio Interchange File (uncompressed format)
WAV	Waveform Audio File (uncompressed format)
MIDI	Musical Instrument Digital Interface (compressed format)
MP3	Audio file format based on MPEG technology (compressed format)
WMA	Windows Media Audio (compressed format)

Check your understanding

Tested

1 Name one method you can use to transfer video files from one mobile phone to another.

2 Why is it important that you optimise a video file before transferring it across the internet?

3 What is a codec?

4 Identify three file formats suitable for distribution of video files across the internet.

5 Identify three file formats suitable for distribution of sound files across the internet.

6 Why is it necessary to convert sound waves from analogue to digital format for storage on an electronic medium?

7 Why do mobile phones and digital cameras come with expansion slots for storage of video files, sound files and digital photographs?

8 Expand the following acronyms: FLA, MPEG, AVI, MIDI, AIF, WAV.

9 Give one advantage of distributing video files between mobile phones through Bluetooth as opposed to using the Multimedia Messaging Service (MMS).

Go online for answers

Online

Digital video planning, production and distribution

Digital video planning

A plan for a movie should be in the format of a storyboard that shows:

- details of any title or credit screens
- a timeline for the digital video, including:
  - a description of any movie clip to be included and how long it is
  - a description of any still image to be included and how long it will appear for
- the name and duration of any audio file or audio effect to be included
- any special effects such as transitions or video effects.

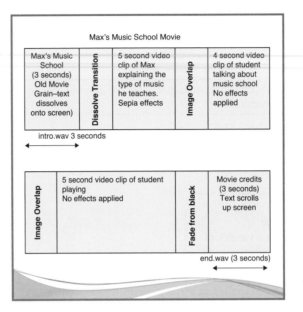

Max's Music School Movie

| Max's Music School (3 seconds) Old Movie Grain–text dissolves onto screen) | Dissolve Transition | 5 second video clip of Max explaining the type of music he teaches. Sepia effects | Image Overlap | 4 second video clip of student talking about music school No effects applied |

intro.wav 3 seconds

| Image Overlap | 5 second video clip of student playing No effects applied | Fade from black | Movie credits (3 seconds) Text scrolls up screen |

end.wav (3 seconds)

Exam tip

Consider the need for careful planning of content and the importance of keeping digital video files limited in size, especially if they are to be distributed over the internet.

Digital video production

Most software used for producing digital videos will allow you to:

- add transitions between movie clips to affect the way you move from one movie clip to another

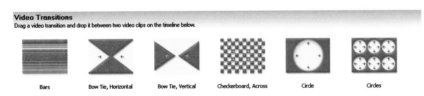

Video Transitions
Drag a video transition and drop it between two video clips on the timeline below.

Bars   Bow Tie, Horizontal   Bow Tie, Vertical   Checkerboard, Across   Circle   Circles

- add effects to movie clips to change the way a movie clip is presented on the screen

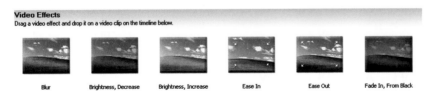

Video Effects
Drag a video effect and drop it on a video clip on the timeline below.

Blur   Brightness, Decrease   Brightness, Increase   Ease In   Ease Out   Fade In, From Black

- split or trim movie clips into smaller, more manageable clips, for example, so that different effects can be added to different scenes
- reposition movie clips on the movie timeline

- add audio files
- add title and credit screens at the beginning or end of the movie and before individual movie clips or still images.

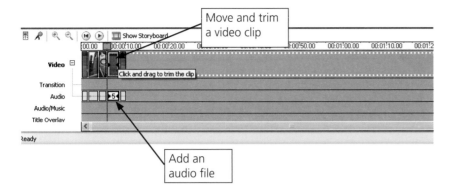

Move and trim a video clip

Add an audio file

Digital video distribution

How your movie is to be distributed will impact on how you save it. The software will give you export tools for you to choose the correct settings. Possible methods of distribution include:

- playback on your computer
- CD distribution
- email distribution
- internet distribution
- digital video camera playback.

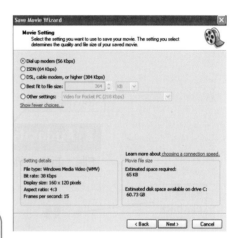

Exam tip

Consider why the method of distribution needs to be specified when saving a digital video file; e.g. if you are sending your video across the internet you need to specify if it is being transferred via dial-up, ISDN or LAN as different protocols and compressions are used.

Check your understanding

1 List three items that should be identified in a storyboard for a digital movie file.
2 Explain the following terms in relation to editing digital videos:
   a) timeline
   b) trim
   c) transitions.
3 Identify two elements that could be added to the timeline of a digital movie.
4 Identify three ways a digital video can be distributed to its audience.
5 Explain why planning is important when producing a movie that will eventually be included on a webpage.
6 Give one reason why it is important that you consider the method of distribution before saving a digital movie.

Go online for answers

Digital sound production and distribution

Digital sound production

Most software produced for developing and editing digital sound files allows you to:

● record new sound files
● play back, pause, fast forward, rewind and stop playing recorded sound files
● import existing sound files for editing
● adjust the volume of a recording
● delete part of a recording
● add effects – e.g. fade in and fade out – to a sound recording.

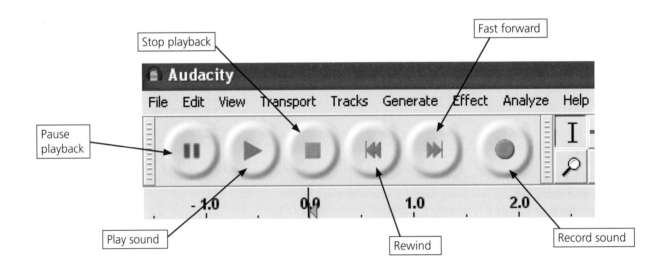

Stop playback

Fast forward

Pause playback

Play sound

Rewind

Record sound

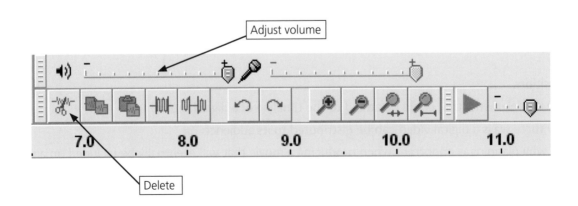

Adjust volume

Delete

Digital sound distribution

Most digital sound editing applications allow you to export and save a
digital sound file in a variety of formats after you have completed editing
it. Compressed and uncompressed file formats are often supported.

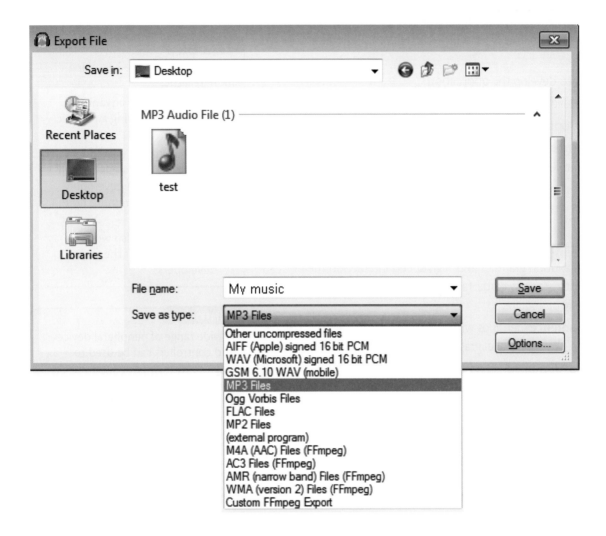

Exam tip

Think carefully about why digital sound files need to be compressed
before they can be distributed over the internet.

Check your understanding

1 Identify three ways digital sound files can be edited using appropriate software.

2 Identify two items of hardware that could be used for the recording of digital sound files.

3 Give one reason why both compressed and uncompressed file formats are often supported in digital sound editing applications.

4 Why is it important that digital sound editing applications allow users to export their sound files in a variety of formats?

5 Identify two uncompressed file formats that could be used when exporting digital audio files.

6 Identify two compressed file formats that could be used when exporting edited digital audio files.

Go online for answers

Online

Game development and game genres

How games are developed

Revised

Large teams of people are involved in developing computer games. Teams can include:

- programmers to develop the application
- musicians to develop the soundtrack
- artists to develop the graphics
- hardware designers to develop peripherals and controllers to match the gaming and ICT skill levels of the users with the demands of the game.

Game developers need to consider the following factors when designing computer games:

- The game platform is the hardware and software needed to play the game. High-resolution graphics and high-speed interaction mean that high-quality graphics cards, fast processors and good-quality peripherals may be required.
- The **target audience** identifies who the game is aimed at; this has an impact on the game interface, graphic quality, language and controllers.
- The method of distribution can be via CD-ROM, DVD-ROM or download, amongst others.
- The game cost is affected by how much it costs to develop and distribute to end users and the need for specialised controllers. The game cost will have an impact on how successful the game is.

Exam tip

Game controllers are becoming more realistic.

- Think about the advantages to the user of using a realistic controller.
- How have game developers considered the needs of their customers when developing controllers that require no ICT skills?
- How does this also work to the advantage of the game developers?

Exam tip

A wide range of peripheral devices and controllers can be used to interact with computer games. Consider carefully the most appropriate devices for a variety of game genres and be able to identify specific devices for the genres listed in the specification.

Gaming platforms

Revised

The PC remains a popular gaming platform.

Hand-held gaming devices include:

- iPod touch
- N-gage
- Nintendo DS and DS Lite
- PSP
- mobile phone and PDA.

Dedicated games consoles include:

- Dreamcast
- Nintendo GameCube
- Nintendo Wii
- Sony PlayStation
- X Box 360.

Game genres

Revised

A game genre identifies a number of characteristics and game plays (or sets of rules) shared by a group of games. Games very often take on the characteristics of more than one genre.

Action Games	Adventure Games
Time-crucial scenario Slow reactions can mean loss of points/lives	Solve puzzles Outcome can affect path taken through game
Game Genres	
Puzzle Games	Role Play Games (RPG)
Time restriction on task completion Increasing levels of difficulty	Play in persona of game character

Exam tip

Think carefully about the differences between game genres. For example, adventure games and puzzle games require the user to complete puzzles but puzzle games only allow the user to move on to the next level when they have successfully completed their current level.

Game play

Revised

When designing a computer game, developers outline the **game play**, which includes:

- the **rules** of the game, e.g. how points can be scored
- the various **pathways** through the game, e.g. how the user can move from one level in a game to the next, possibly through the use of scoring
- the script of the game (normally using a **storyboard**)
- how the user **interacts** with the game (e.g. what controls to use, what **feedback** to expect).

Check your understanding

Tested

1 Identify four different teams of people that may be involved in the development of computer games.
2 List two advantages to the user of interacting with computer games using realistic games controllers.
3 Name two methods a developer can use to distribute games to the general public.
4 List three examples of hardware platforms used to play computer games.
5 List four game genres.
6 List two differences between puzzle and adventure games.
7 Identify two characteristics of role play games.
8 Explain two elements that should be included in the game play of a new computer game before it can be developed.

Go online for answers

Online

Trends in computer gaming

Hardware developments

Revised

A wide range of devices provide user interaction with computer games:

- **Haptic peripheral** devices provide sensory feedback to the user in the form of vibration.
- Joysticks allow for multidirectional movement and button input.
- Concept keyboards have predesigned overlays that allow the user to select a variety of options when interacting with the game.
- Touch screens allow the user to select options easily on screen.
- Specialised keyboards provide basic controls on some hand-held consoles.
- QWERTY keyboards can be used to control some basic computer games.
- Specialised controllers, such as tennis racquets and steering wheels, provide interaction with more complex games.
- Touch-sensitive devices, e.g. dance mats, can be used to provide input into some games.

Technology has had an impact on the quality and type of games and consoles available today. Increases in processing speed and graphic resolution has improved the quality of games available on the market today.

> ### Exam tip
>
> A computer game is the electronic presentation of any game that involves interaction between the user and a processor using an electronic device that provides feedback to the user.
>
> Consider how computer games might continue to develop in the future:
>
> - How might users interact with the games?
> - How might games be distributed?
> - What impact might this have on the technology needed to play these games?

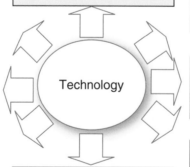

Increased processing power increased game responsiveness

Mobile gaming devices increased popularity of gaming among all age groups

Realistic or natural interactions more natural interactions with games consoles

Smaller technology more hand-held gaming devices

Technology

Improved graphics cards more realistic graphics

Improved internet access e.g. broadband more online gaming

Improved internet access e.g. broadband increased gaming on demand (GoD)

Improved internet access e.g. Wi-Fi increased social gaming

Developments in consoles and game genres

Revised

- **Games consoles** provide high-quality graphics cards and high-speed processing. They may provide internet access and the ability to play Blu-ray disks.

- **Online gaming** allows users to play computer games online with other people around the world. They are normally played using a PC but hand-held consoles provide the same facility. High-speed internet access is required to support graphics and sound transmission.

- A massive multiplayer online role-play game (**MMPORG**) often requires subscription to a dedicated website. Game players may not know the others they are playing against.

- **Social gaming** is normally played via a social networking site and against people who are members of your 'friends' list.

- **Mobile gaming** uses communication devices to play computer games. They are often pre-installed on the device or they can be downloaded and installed by the user.

- **Altered reality gaming** superimposes computer-generated images onto images from the users' current environment.

- **Peripheral-free game play** uses natural movements to interact with computer games. This helps make games more appealing to the general public.

- **Casual gaming** involves basic computer games that require little gaming or ICT skill.

- **Training games** use high-quality 3D graphics to train specialised staff.

Exam tip

It is important that you take into consideration the impact that **internet technologies** have had on each of these gaming trends. For example, **Bluetooth**, **WAP** and **Wi-Fi** have affected the use of **mobile phones** and **hand-held consoles** as online gaming tools.

Check your understanding

Tested

1 Identify two other facilities many games consoles now provide in addition to allowing users to play computer games.

2 List three devices that can be used to allow users to interact with computer games.

3 Identify two ways technology has improved the quality of computer games.

4 Explain how haptic devices differ from standard game controllers.

5 Explain two ways improved internet connectivity has impacted on electronic gaming.

6 Give two reasons why peripheral-free game play will help increase the popularity of computer gaming.

7 List one difference between MMPORG and social gaming.

8 Identify two professions that could make use of training games and in each case give an example of how they might be used.

9 Explain what is meant by 'altered reality gaming'.

Go online for answers

Online

Computer game production

Computer game proposal document

Before creating a proposal for a computer game, it is important to establish:

- what the game is expected to do – a description of the game
- what type of **interactions** the user will have with the game, e.g. rollover buttons, button clicks
- what sort of feedback users are expected to get from the game, e.g. text boxes, dialogue boxes, auditory feedback
- how the **scoring mechanism** will allow users to score points in the game.

A computer game proposal should contain:

- a description of the **target audience**
- details of the **game genre**
- details about the **game play**
- a **storyboard** detailing the various elements of the game.

When specifying the target audience, consideration should be given to:

- the age of the audience – this might help determine colours and type of graphics
- specific characteristics of the audience – e.g. you might want to include interests or logos that apply to the target audience in your game.

The storyboard should include details of:

- background colour and text colour
- type and location of graphics
- location of key elements such as:
  - ■ title screen
  - ■ main menu
  - ■ screen titles
  - ■ game instructions
  - ■ game elements
  - ■ exit button
  - ■ help button
  - ■ navigation buttons
  - ■ scoring mechanism
  - ■ location of graphics and animations
- **feedback** to be given
- content of the **help facility**.

Game Proposal for Name the Peripheral ICT game

Target Audience:
The game is aimed at GCSE students who will use it to revise input and output devices for their GCSE examination.

Game Genre:
The game will take a quiz format.

Game Play:
The game main menu will offer the user two options when they start up the game: Name that Input Device or Name that Output Device.

In each game, the user will be presented with a series of pictures of different peripheral devices. The user needs to name each device and spell the device name correctly to score points in the game. For every peripheral correctly identified, the user will hear applause and will get a message on screen saying 'Correct' and they will score 5 points. For every device incorrectly named ...

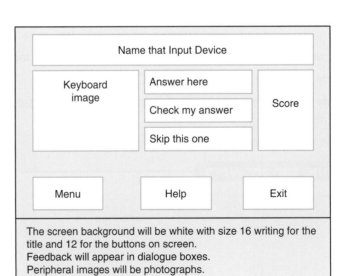

Producing a computer game

Revised

Most games include the following elements:

- programming instructions
- **interaction** in the form of **rollover images** and/or **button clicks**
- user **feedback** in the form of messages
- graphics in an appropriate format.

Applications such as Microsoft PowerPoint allow you to add programming elements to your game using the Developer Tab.

Radio buttons, action buttons and other controls in Microsoft PowerPoint can be used to control a basic computer game.

One method of providing feedback is to use programming instructions to create dialogue boxes with user feedback.

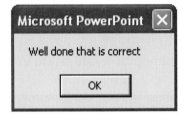

Graphics should be:

- appropriate for the audience
- of good quality
- supported by the platform the game is to be played on.

User guide or help facility

Revised

A user guide or help facility should be available to the user at all times throughout the game. At the very least, it should include:

- the rules of the game
- instructions on how to control or play the game
- explanation of any feedback the user might get
- instructions on how to exit the game.

Check your understanding

Tested

1 Identify three elements you should include in a game proposal.
2 Explain what is meant by the 'target audience' of a computer game.
3 List two examples of feedback game players can receive when interacting with a computer game.
4 Identify three elements that should be included in the user guide or help facility of a computer game.
5 List three items that should be included in the storyboard for a computer game.
6 Why is it important that the storyboard includes descriptions of text, font, colour of text, etc.?

Go online for answers

Online

Testing and evaluating computer games

Testing a computer game

Revised

Like all applications, computer games should be tested before they are released to the public. Tests carried out on computer games should at the very least ensure that:

- all pathways through the game can be accessed
- the scoring mechanism works correctly
- any feedback is in a format that is easy for the user to understand
- instructions are easy to understand and can be easily accessed by the user.

Evaluating a computer game

Revised

Before a computer game is made available to the public it is important that a detailed evaluation of the game is carried out to help ensure:

- the suitability of the interface for the target audience:
  - Is the language used appropriate?
  - If the game is aimed at small children, is the text large and easy to read?
  - Are the graphics appropriate?
- the accuracy of the score counter
- the instructions in the help facility are easy to follow.

What makes a good computer game?

Revised

Popular computer games tend to:

- be appropriately priced
- be available on the correct platform (or a variety of platforms)
- use language that is appropriate for the target audience
- incorporate game play that is appropriate for the target audience
- have appropriate peripherals that enhance the game play experience
- have technical support readily available (through user documentation, discussion forums, gaming magazines, etc.)
- be distributed using appropriate media, e.g., GoD (Game on Demand), online, CD-ROM or DVD-ROM.

Check your understanding

Tested

1 Identify three elements of a computer game you should test to help ensure the game works correctly.
2 Give one reason why appropriate technical support is so important when developing a computer game to be used by other people.
3 Give one reason why it is important to consider the target audience when evaluating a computer game.
4 Why is it important to game developers that they make their computer games available on a variety of platforms?

Go online for answers

Online

Website development and multimedia components

How websites are developed

Revised

- A website is a set of **HyperText Markup Language (HTML)** documents that can be viewed on the World Wide Web.
- HTML documents can contain a combination of text and other multimedia objects such as video, sound, animated images and digital photographs.
- Webpages are normally linked using **hyperlinks**. A hyperlink is text or an image that directs you to another webpage or website when you click on it.

A website can be developed by individuals or teams of people, depending on the purpose of the website. Website designers need to consider the following when designing and developing websites:

- the target audience, which identifies who the website is aimed at; this will have an impact on the interface, graphic type and language
- the purpose of the website, whether it is to be used for advertising, passing on information, selling something or education.

> **Exam tip**
>
> Think about how the purpose of a website might affect its content; e.g. if it is to be an online shop, it should be a secure website with https in the web address.

Website planning

Revised

Website development plans should include:

- a description of the target audience
- the purpose of the website
- a navigation diagram to show the number of webpages in the website and how the webpages are linked
- a storyboard that includes details about the content of each webpage:
  - the position and function of graphics, animations, videos and other digital assets
  - the colour scheme for each webpage
  - the location of navigation elements.

Website Planning Document for Simon's Skateboard Club

Target Audience:
This website is aimed at teenagers who are members of Simon's Club and others who are interested in skateboarding and skater clothing.

Purpose:
The website will provide information about the location of skateboard rinks, skateboard designs, skateboarding competitions and skateboard and skater clothing outlets in the local area.

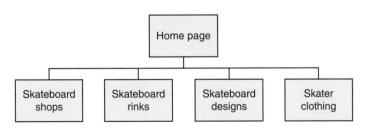

> **Exam tip**
>
> Consider how you might show a link to another website in the website navigation diagram.

Storyboard

Revised

What makes a good website? Consider these points in your storyboard:

- A good website can be easily navigated.
- A good website loads quickly.
- A good website will have a consistent layout in terms of navigation and the look and feel in each webpage.

The storyboard should contain enough detail to allow someone else to produce the webpages.

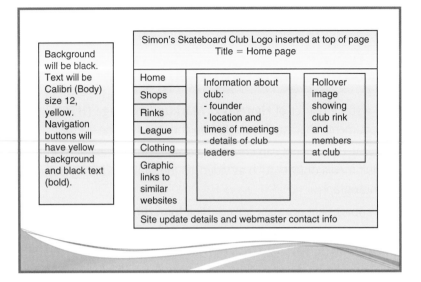

Multimedia components

Revised

Websites can contain a variety of multimedia components. These include:

- graphic elements – **JPG**, **GIF** and **PNG** are examples of suitable graphic file formats.
- sound files – **WAV**, **AIF**, **MP3** and **WMA** are appropriate sound file formats.
- video files – **AVI**, **MPEG**, **MOV**, **WMV** and **SWF** are suitable video file formats.
- animations – **FLA** and **GIF** are appropriate animation file formats.

Always make the appropriate plugins available for the web user so they can view the files you have added to your webpage. A plugin is an additional piece of software that can be downloaded to add extra features to an application.

Check your understanding

Tested

1 Expand the acronym HTML.

2 What is meant by the term 'hyperlink'?

3 Give two examples of the ways hyperlinks can be provided on a webpage.

4 List two examples of multimedia components that can be added to webpages.

5 Identify three elements that should be included in a website storyboard.

6 List appropriate file types for the following multimedia components if they are to be included in a website: animation, video and sound file.

7 Explain what is meant by the term 'plugin'.

Go online for answers

Online

Software features and site management

Web authoring packages allow users to create and edit webpages and websites using some or all of the tools mentioned below.

Page formatting tools allow the web developer to customise the look of pages they are creating:

● An image can be added to the webpage background.

● The background colour and text colours can be set.

● The colours used to identify hyperlinks can be changed.

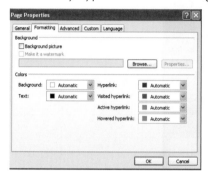

Exam tip

Consider why it may not always be a good idea to use a graphic in the background of a webpage.

A template is a pre-designed webpage that contains some basic text and graphics that can be edited by the user. Text font, text size and text style can all be changed to enhance the presentation of the webpage.

The developer can add the following elements to a webpage:

● hyperlinks – buttons, text, graphics that can be clicked on to take the user to another webpage, website or document

● hotspots – sections of a large graphic that are hyperlinked to another webpage, website or document

● multimedia components – video, graphics, animation and sound

● document links – hyperlinks that link to documents within the website folder (the documents can be viewed online or downloaded)

● navigation menus – links to each of the pages available in the website

● layout features:

■ **framesets** – a group of pages that can be displayed at the same time; they look like one page in the web browser

Hotspot

- **layers** – containers for text and other multimedia elements on a webpage
- tables – data on a webpage organised into rows and columns.

Web authoring packages contain the following views that help the developer:

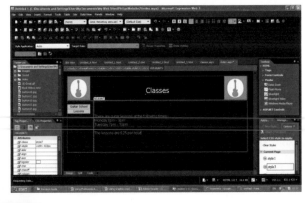

- **Design view** allows the web developer to add text and multimedia elements to the webpage they are developing.
- **Preview mode** allows the user to view the webpage in a web browser.
- **Code view** allows the user to see and edit the HTML code used to create the webpage they are developing.

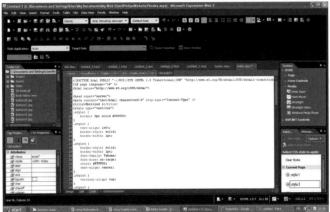

Site management

Revised

Websites can sometimes contain many pages and multimedia elements.
To help keep the website easy to manage, you should:

- create separate folders for images and other multimedia elements
- use appropriate file names for multimedia elements and webpages
- make the home page easily identifiable, e.g. by saving it as index.html.

Navigation

Revised

The website should be easy for the user to navigate and the user should easily be able to get back to the home page at any time.

Navigation can be provided in a variety of formats:

- **vertical navigation** – hyperlinks are listed down one side of the webpage

Vertical navigation

- **horizontal navigation** – hyperlinks are listed across the page (normally close to the top of the page)

- ordered lists – users can click on hyperlinks that provide a further series of options to choose from
- **tabs** – the pages are categorised and listed under general headings that are displayed in a tab menu

- **sitemap** – a webpage lists the content of the website and hyperlinks to each page (like the index of a book)
- **breadcrumb trail** – a list of pages visited and the sequence in which they were viewed (normally along the top of the webpage)

Check your understanding Tested

1 Identify one problem with adding a background image to a webpage.
2 Explain the difference between the following methods of viewing webpage content: code view, preview mode, design view.
3 Give one reason why a website developer may want to edit the HTML code created for a webpage.
4 Explain the difference between breadcrumb trail navigation and a sitemap.
5 Give one advantage of using breadcrumb trail navigation.
6 Give one reason for using folders to help organise the multimedia components used in a website.
7 Explain the difference between vertical navigation and horizontal navigation.

Go online for answers Online

Testing and evaluating websites

Testing a website

If a website is to be fully tested it should be viewed using a number of different web browsers.

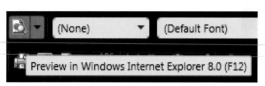

Website developers need to carry out tests on at least the following elements of a webpage before it can be published on the Internet:

- All hyperlinks should be thoroughly tested to ensure the hyperlink takes the user to the correct webpage, website or document.
- The time taken to load webpages should be considered; if a webpage takes too long to load, the viewer may not wait for it.
- All images should be viewed to ensure that they display on the webpage.
- All videos, animations and sound files should be checked to ensure they play correctly.

Exam tip

Consider why it is important for a web developer to test a website using more than one web browser.

Exam tip

The examiner could ask you to identify problems with a completed webpage. For example, you should be able to give appropriate reasons why a hyperlink does not work or a graphic does not display correctly.

Evaluating a website

The following elements need to be considered when evaluating a website:

- graphics and use of colour
  - Is the file format appropriate?
  - Are the graphics good quality, relevant and appropriately placed?
- download time for multimedia webpages – do the pages load quickly or is there a delay while large graphics or other multimedia elements are downloaded?
- successful and broken hyperlinks – do all hyperlinks take the user to the correct location or display the correct documents?
- ease of navigation
  - How well laid out is the site?
  - Can the user easily return to the home page or top of the page?
- content
  - Is the content appropriate for the purpose of the website?
  - Does it meet the users' requirements?

Check your understanding

1. Explain the term 'preview in web browser'.
2. Say why it is a good idea to test a website using more than one web browser.
3. Give one reason why a website may look different in a web browser from how it looks when viewed using the software used to create it.
4. Explain the term 'broken hyperlink'.
5. Why is it important that a website allows a user to easily return to the home page at all times?
6. List two ways a user can return to the home page on a website.
7. Give one reason why a graphic image may not appear on a webpage when it is previewed in a web browser.

Go online for answers

Input devices

Input devices

Revised

Keyboard

- uses a standard layout, referred to as QWERTY
- depends on the human operator for speed of input
- is prone to human error since all data is keyed-in
- is used to enter text into the computer.

Some keyboards (e.g. EPOS and ATM) are specially designed for specific applications. They may have fewer keys and an emphasis on numeric keys.

Concept keyboards have keys with pictures or words that can be programmed to carry out specific instructions.

Tracker pad

- known as a 'touch-sensitive' pad – it can sense touch from a finger
- used as an alternative to a mouse on a laptop computer
- ideal for a portable device as it can be used in a confined space.

Movement on the pad controls the cursor, which allows the user to select options from menus, select icons and position the cursor.

Exam tips

- You need to learn four features of each device.
- Look out for common features. 'Minimal training required' is a feature for many of these devices.
- By learning features, you can answer questions on advantages and disadvantages of input devices. For example, 'No additional hardware (such as a keyboard or mouse) required' is a feature and an advantage of a touch screen.

Mouse

- is also referred to as a 'pointing device'
- is easy to use and inexpensive compared to other input devices
- is designed to fit under the human hand
- can contain two or three buttons which are used to make selections on the screen.

Experienced users may find using a mouse slow compared to using '**hot keys**'. For example they might prefer to use Ctrl and P rather than selecting Print from menus and options.

Some mice use a mouse ball and built-in movement sensors. Other mice use infrared or wireless technology. A tracker ball is an alternative to a mouse.

Joystick

- allows the user to control an object on the screen by manoeuvring a small lever in different directions
- senses movements, which are converted to co-ordinates
- usually has pre-programmed buttons to allow actions to be carried out
- is used to play computer games.

Touch screen

- a special type of screen which reacts to human touch
- minimal user training required
- no additional hardware (such as a keyboard or mouse) required
- more expensive than a normal LCD screen
- used in banks, tourist offices, museums and supermarkets
- used in hand-held games consoles, PDAs and mobile telephones.

When the user's finger touches the screen, vertical and horizontal beams of light are sensed and then converted into a co-ordinate. You can drag your finger across the screen to perform 'drag and drop' operations.

Microphone

- designed to input sound or human voice into a computer system
- used in voice-recognition applications
- natural form of communication for humans
- background noise can interfere with spoken words
- can record music and store in digital format.

The spoken word can be converted to text or the computer can interpret spoken commands. The user can record and store words and phrases in a database which can be used to recognise words and phrases in future.

Voice recognition is helpful for users with less mobility: they can use their voice instead of a mouse or other input device.

Digital camera

- stores pictures on a **memory card**
- a small liquid crystal display (LCD) screen is attached to view pictures taken immediately
- pictures can be downloaded to a computer connected to the camera with a USB cable or a wireless connection.

Memory cards have a typical capacity of 4 GB, which allows around 1000 pictures to be stored in medium resolution.

Digital cameras can also capture short video clips that last a couple of minutes.

Scanner

A scanner converts a hard copy of pictures or text into a digital image. Beams of bright light are passed over the image, which is recognised as a series of dots on a page.

- Once an image has been scanned, it can be saved and edited using standard software.
- If text is scanned it can be recognised by a word processor using optical character recognition (OCR) software. Text can then be edited and saved electronically.

The quality of the image scanned is measured in dots per inch (dpi). Cheap scanners can scan at 2400 x 4800 dpi but only up to A4 in size. The greater the dpi, the greater the resolution.

Graphics digitiser

- a flat electronic sensitive surface that captures the image drawn with a **stylus** pen
- allows the user to record a hand-drawn image in a computer system
- the image drawn can be imported to a graphics package for further editing.

Check your understanding   Tested

1 Identify three features of a digital camera.
2 State two benefits of using a touch screen.
3 Complete the table to show which input devices have the features listed.

Device	Feature
	Allows the user to record a hand-drawn image onto a computer system
	Converts a hard copy of pictures or text into a digital image
	Has keys with pictures or words
	Senses touch from your finger

Go online for answers   Online

Output devices

Visual display unit (VDU)

- A visual display unit (VDU) displays information or output from the computer on the screen.
- A **pixel** is the smallest area on the screen that can be edited. A picture is made up of a number of pixels.
- Screen **resolution** is a measure of the quality of the image on the screen. The more pixels, the higher the resolution.
- The cost of the monitor increases as size and resolution get bigger.
- An LCD screen is much lighter and smaller than a typical desktop cathode ray tube (CRT) screen.
- LCD screens do not require as much power, making them more energy efficient.
- Some VDUs have inbuilt speakers and a microphone, making them suitable for multimedia uses.
- Modern VDUs have an inbuilt filtering system to help reduce eyestrain.

Impact printer

The print head is made up of a series of pins laid out in rows and columns (a matrix). The print head strikes an ink ribbon, leaving an impression on the page. Characters are formed as a series of dots when the tiny pins strike the ink ribbon. The more pins in the print head, the better the quality of the printer.

An impact (dot-matrix) printer:

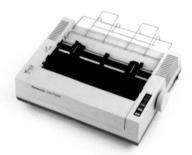

- is useful when organisations need to produce carbon copy printouts such as invoices or delivery notes
- prints only in one colour
- costs less to produce multiple copies of data (using the carbon copy method)
- produces low-quality print compared to a laser printer
- can be noisy in the workplace.

Laser printer

A laser printer is a non-impact printer which uses a toner kit to produce printouts. Some laser printers are manufactured as three-in-one devices to include a scanner, a photocopier and/or fax capabilities.

Laser printers usually have their own memory where pages are temporarily stored before printing.

A laser printer:

- can print in black and white or colour
- is suitable for high-volume printing, such as in a school network
- produces excellent print quality compared to other printers
- works at greater speeds than other printers.

Inkjet printer

An inkjet printer is a non-impact printer which uses black and coloured ink cartridges to produce printouts. The ink is heated and then sprayed through the many nozzles or jets in the print head to form characters or images. An inkjet printer:

- can print in black and white or colour
- is suitable for home use to print photographs and small volumes of documents
- has high-quality print which slows down the speed of output
- is slow at producing output compared to a laser printer.

Plotter

Some plotters use electronically controlled pens while others are 'penless' plotters (raster plotters). A plotter:

- produces high-quality accurate and detailed diagrams
- is used by architects, surveyors, pattern makers and engineers
- can use a variety of paper sizes, such as A0
- can draw characters of different sizes and different fonts to be added to the drawings.

Speaker

- small internal speakers are standard in computers
- provides sound output through the sound card from a computer
- can output music as well as the spoken word
- is useful for visually impaired users
- can draw attention to an input error (e.g. a 'beep' is output when a barcode is incorrectly scanned).

Exam tips

- You need to learn four features of each device.
- Look out for common features. 'Can print in colour or black and white' is a feature of many of these devices.
- By learning features, you can also answer questions on advantages and disadvantages of output devices. For example, 'Suitable for high-volume printing such as in a school network' is a feature and an advantage of a laser printer.

Check your understanding   Tested

1 Identify three features of an impact printer.
2 State two benefits of using a plotter to produce hardcopy drawings.
3 Complete the table to show which output devices have the features listed.

Device	Feature
	Can be useful for visually impaired users
	Contains nozzles or jets that spray ink
	Uses a toner kit to produce printouts
	Displays information or output from the computer onto the screen

Go online for answers   Online

Data storage devices

Data storage devices

Memory and storage capacity on a computer is measured in bits and bytes. A bit (or *binary digit*) is the smallest unit of storage on a computer. It is a 1 or 0.

Unit	Value
1 byte	8 bits (a character is usually 8 bits in size)
1 kilobyte (KB)	1024 bytes (approx. 1000 bytes)
1 megabyte (MB)	1024 kilobytes (approx. 1000 KB)
1 gigabyte (GB)	1024 megabytes (approx. 1000 MB)
1 terabyte (TB)	1024 gigabytes (approx. 1000 GB)

Data storage devices allow programs and data to be stored permanently. External storage devices are grouped into:

- magnetic disks
- optical devices
- magnetic tapes
- USB flash drives.

Details about network and online storage are given on page 68.

Hard disks

- the main storage device of a computer system
- a number of rigid disks stacked on top of one another; each disk has two surfaces, consisting of a number of tracks and sectors
- a read/write head for each surface
- access speeds are faster than a CD drive.

The hard disk drive is contained in a sealed unit to protect it against damage from dirt and dust.

Internal hard disks are used to permanently store the operating system, all application software and user data on a PC or network.

External hard drives are portable with a high storage capacity. They can be attached using a USB cable. These are suitable for small-scale backup of data.

Optical disks

Compact disks (CDs) have a typical capacity of 700 MB. They are portable media, classified in the following ways.

CD-ROM (CD-Read only memory):

- Data is burned onto the surface of the disk using a laser beam which makes small indentations known as pits.
- The disks are supplied with information, such as music and software, already stored on them.
- The user can read data from it but *not* write to it.
- The cost is determined by the application stored on it.

CD-R (CD-Recordable):

- The disks are supplied blank.
- The user can record data onto the disk *once* only (a 'write once read many' (WORM) disk).
- Data can be read from the disk as often as required.
- They are used to store data or music or for small-scale backup on a PC.

CD-RW (CD-Rewriteable):

- The disks are supplied blank.
- The user can record data onto the disk, erase it and rewrite it many times.
- CD-RWs are more expensive than CD-Rs.

DVD (digital versatile disk or digital video disk) is similar in appearance to a CD but is encoded differently so it needs a different drive (a DVD drive) to read and write.

- A DVD drive can also read CDs.
- Typical storage capacity is 5 GB for a single-layer DVD and up to 17 GB for a double-sided, dual-layer DVD.
- DVDs are used to store large amounts of data and films.
- DVDs can be read from and written to. DVD-Rs can be written once. DVD-RWs are rewriteable.

Blu-ray disks:

- Have a much larger storage capacity than DVDs.
- Can be used for recording high-definition television without loss of quality.
- Can store digitally encoded video and audio data.
- Storage capacity is around 50 GB (about ten times the amount of information that can be stored on a single-layer DVD).

Magnetic tape streamers

- A tape streamer reads and writes data stored on magnetic tape – digital audio tape (DAT).
- Data is stored in blocks and there is a gap between each block.
- Transfer of data is slow because magnetic tape uses serial access.
- Networks use a tape streamer linked to the server to make backups of the hard disk.
- Magnetic tape is an inexpensive way to store large amounts of data.

USB flash drives

- Flash drives are also referred to as '**pen drives**'.
- They consist of an inbuilt circuit board and a USB connector.
- The flash drive becomes active when plugged into a USB port.
- The USB connection also forms the power supply.
- Flash drives are physically compact compared to a CD or DVD.
- They are portable devices that use low power consumption.

- They work on the principle of 'plug and play'.
- Cost is linked to the capacity of the USB flash drive.

Check your understanding
Tested

1 Complete the following paragraph using each word only once:

kilobyte   byte   bit   character

A _____ is the smallest unit of memory. 8 bits make up 1 _____.
A _____ is usually 1 byte in size. A _____ is made up of 1024 bytes.

2 List these units in order of size: kilobyte, byte, megabyte, gigabyte.

3 Identify three features of:

   a) a hard drive   **b)** a Blu-ray disk.

4 State two benefits of using a USB flash drive for GCSE coursework.

Go online for answers
Online

Memory

Revised

Memory

One of the main components of the CPU is the memory (main memory). The main memory is divided into categories:

- ROM (read-only memory)
- RAM (random-access memory)
- cache memory.

ROM (read-only memory)

- This type of memory can be read from but not written to.
- Programs stored on ROM are permanent, therefore ROM is non-volatile.
- This type of memory is used to store the 'booting up' program for the Windows operating system, which runs automatically when the computer is switched on.

RAM (random-access memory)

- This type of memory can be read from or written to.
- It is volatile, which means the contents of the memory are lost when the machine is switched off.
- It is used to hold the current application programs and data that the user is working with.
- All programs and data, including those currently in use, are usually held permanently on the hard disk.
- The size of RAM can influence the speed of the processor; the larger the RAM capacity, the faster the processor.

Cache memory

- Cache (pronounced 'cash') memory is a special form of memory located close to the processor.
- It is similar to RAM in that instructions can be read from or written to cache.
- It is small in capacity compared to RAM but offers faster access speeds.
- Its purpose is to store frequently accessed program instructions.

> **Exam tip**
>
> Use appropriate terms when describing ROM and RAM, such as volatile memory (RAM) and non-volatile memory (ROM).

Check your understanding

Tested

1 Identify two uses of RAM.
2 Describe two features of ROM.
3 Which category of memory has the features listed in the table?

Memory	Feature
	Stores frequently accessed program instructions
	Stores the 'booting up' program for the Windows operating system
	Stores the current application programs and user data

Go online for answers

Online

System software

The operating system can be referred to as system software. The main purpose of the operating system is to provide an interface to allow the user to communicate with the computer system. The operating system also manages and controls all of the hardware and software. The main functions of the operating system include:

- interface – allowing communication between the user and the computer
- memory management – allocating internal memory (RAM) to programs and data that the user is currently using; retrieving and storing data on the external memory devices
- resource management – controlling peripheral (input and output) devices and handling user requests for peripheral devices
- execution – 'booting up' the computer when it is switched on
- error handling – dealing with errors that occur when programs are running and communicating the responses to software developers and the user
- system security – checking and controlling user access to programs and data to prevent unauthorised access.

Graphical user interface (GUI) — Revised

A popular **user interface** is a graphical user interface (GUI).

Feature	Description
Windows	• Each folder, program or document opened by a user is displayed in a separate window. • Windows can be minimised or maximised. • The window that is maximised is described as the 'active' window.
Icons	• Small graphics representing a program, file or a tool from a toolbar are 'icons'. • Icons reside on the desktop as shortcuts to folders, programs or documents. • When you double-click an icon, the folder, program or document opens. • Can be customised in appearance and arranged by size or date modified.
Menus	• Menus can be 'pull down' or 'pop up'. • Each menu provides a list of options for the user to select from. • Menus can be customised to show a full list of options (full menu) or a smaller list of options (short menu).
Pointers	• A pointer shows the position of the cursor on the screen. • A typical user controls the pointer using a mouse. • The user can move the pointer over an icon and then use the buttons on the mouse to select and open the folder, program or document.

Other features of a GUI include dialogue boxes, toolbars, buttons and tool tips.

> **Exam tip**
>
> By learning WIMP, you can state four features of a GUI.

Check your understanding — Tested

1 Describe the purpose of an operating system.

2 Identify three features of a typical operating system.

3 Which feature of a GUI fits the descriptions listed in the table?

Feature	Description of feature
	I am a graphic that represents a program, a file or a tool from a toolbar.
	I can be minimised or maximised.
	I provide a list of options for the user to select from.

Go online for answers — Online

Gathering data

The difference between data and information

An information system processes **data** to produce **information**.

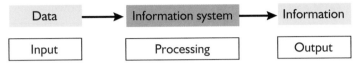

| Data | → | Information system | → | Information |

| Input | | Processing | | Output |

Processing data means taking the values and manipulating them to produce information. Data is raw facts and figures which have not been given a meaning. This list of numbers could be described as a set of data:

85, 60, 65, 90, 70, 50, 40, 77, 60.

Information is data which has been given a meaning or which has been processed in some way to give it meaning. For example, this list of pupil marks is information:

85%, 60%, 65%, 90%, 70%, 50%, 40%, 77%, 60%.

The average mark for the examination is 66.3. This is information which has been created by processing the data.

Form design

Forms are used to collect data.

- Paper-based forms are used to collect data from people and then the data is keyed in to the computer.
- Screen-based forms are developed to be filled out online or on a computer screen.
- The design quality of the form can affect whether or not the correct data is collected.
- The quality of the data collected will have an effect on the information produced.

A form should include:

- a suitable title and instructions which clearly explain the purpose of the form
- a logo (if appropriate)
- a prompt to tell users what data to enter at each part of the form
- a suitable space to enter each item of data
- boxes, tick boxes, option buttons, etc. to make it easier for users to complete the form and help reduce human error.

When designing a form, ensure that:

- The form is divided up into sections.
- The font chosen is suitable for the intended audience.
- The font varies in size to emphasise sections and headings.
- Colour, if it is used, enhances the form and its layout.

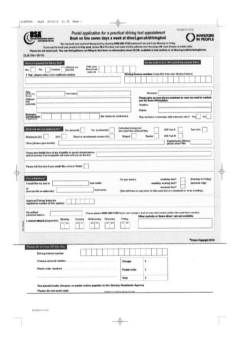

Optical mark recognition (OMR)

Revised

- OMR equipment scans forms which have been filled in using marks or ticks.
- OMR uses light to detect the position of marks on paper.
- Marks are converted to digital data.
- OMR is used for the National Lottery and answer sheets for multiple choice tests.

Exam tip

When explaining the advantages and disadvantages do not use one-word answers such as 'fast'. Always include an explanation as shown.

Advantages of using OMR	Disadvantages of using OMR
• Fast – large amounts of data can be input quickly as OMR allows many documents to be processed one after the other. • Accurate – because data is read directly from the document, it eliminates the possibility of typing errors made by humans. • Data input to a computer using OMR can be analysed to produce high-quality information quickly. • Staff need minimal training in system use as documents are simply passed into a scanner.	• Documents must be kept in good condition – the system may not be able to read creased documents. • OMR input is paper-based and the cost of producing specially designed forms could be high. • Unless the forms are recycled after input, it may not be the most environmentally friendly solution. • The cost of buying OMR equipment can be high.

Optical character recognition (OCR)

Revised

- This technology makes use of an optical scanner.
- It can take paper-based documents and transform them into editable computer files. For example, if you need a digital copy of a document, OCR provides a good alternative to re-typing.
- Most scanners come with an OCR program; it can look at the 'picture' of your document, 'read' the document and convert it to text. The text is editable in a word processor. When a document is scanned using the OCR facility, it is saved as a rich text file (RTF).
- Flat-bed scanners can be used to scan a paper version of a document in the same way as a photocopier.
- OCR is used:
  - by libraries to digitise and preserve old documents and books
  - by the Royal Mail to sort millions of letters every day and speed up mail delivery.

Advantages of using OCR	Disadvantages of using OCR
• Large quantities of text can be input to the computer quickly. • An electronic copy of a paper-based document can be created without re-typing it.	• Documents which are dirty or marked will not be read accurately. • Systems which are highly accurate are expensive. • OCR systems will not produce accurate results when required to scan forms (especially with boxes and check boxes), very small text, shaded photocopies, mathematical formulae or handwritten text.

Check your understanding

Tested

1 Explain how data differs from information.
2 What information other than an average could be obtained from this set of data:

   85, 60, 65, 90, 70, 50, 40, 77, 60?
3 List five features of a well-designed form.
4 List the main advantages of using OMR for capturing data.
5 Describe two uses for OCR.

Go online for answers

Online

Checking data

Data verification

Data **verification** is carried out to ensure that data keyed into a computer has been accurately entered.

One way of performing verification is for the data to be keyed into the computer system twice, by two different computer operators. The computer system compares the two sets of data. Any mismatching data is rejected and re-entered. This ensures that data is transferred accurately and correctly.

Another method of verification is proofreading. This involves reading the typed document and comparing it with the original to make sure that the data entered is accurate and correct.

Have you ever had to change your password on a computer system? Why do you have to type the new password twice? This is a form of data verification.

> **Exam tip**
>
> When answering questions about verification, remember that there are a number of steps:
> - entering the data
> - checking or comparing the two versions
> - rejecting data which does not match.

Data validation techniques

Data collected using a data entry screen must be checked before it is accepted by the computer system. Checking data to ensure that it is acceptable and sensible is called **validation**.

Data validation is performed when data is input. It ensures that the data is present, of the correct type, in the correct range and of the correct length. The computer system automatically validates data input and outputs an error message, if necessary, to inform the user of errors.

Presence check

A **presence check** ensures that some data has been entered into an area on the form. This check means that important data is not omitted. This is common in database applications.

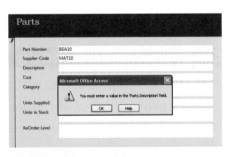

In this case, the user has not entered data into the Description field of the form. An error message is displayed as a result of the validation process.

Length check

A **length check** ensures that entered data is of the correct length. For example, the Part Number may have a length check to ensure that it is six characters long.

Type check

A **type check** ensures that the data entered is of the correct format.

There is a range of data types:

- numeric – data takes on a numeric value and can be used in calculations
- text – data can be made up of letters or letters and numbers
- date – data takes on a value which is formatted as a date or time
- Boolean – data can take only two values, for example, Yes and No, True and False or 0 and 1
- currency – data represents money values.

Format check

A **format check** ensures that data is entered in a particular format. For example, the Supplier Code text field is assigned an input mask that requires the user to enter three letters followed by three numbers (AAA000). The database will not allow data to be entered in any other format.

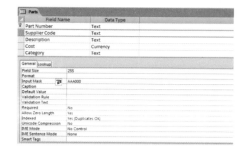

Range check

A **range check** ensures that data entered is within a given range, for example:

- A customer number may take a value between 1 and 500.
- A pupil grade can take a value between 'A' and 'E'.

In this Excel spreadsheet, there is a range check to ensure that values entered into cell C3 are in the range 0–1000.

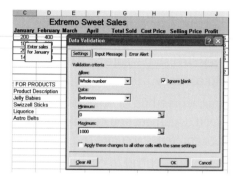

The purpose of a check digit

Revised

A **check digit** is added to the end of a code. The code is used in a calculation and the check digit is recalculated. If the results of the calculation do not match the check digit, an error message appears. The code will have to be input again.

Check digits are found on the ISBN on the back of a book and at the end of the Universal Product Code (UPC) or barcode on items in supermarkets.

Check your understanding

Tested

1 What is the purpose of data verification?
2 Name two methods of verification.
3 When is data validation carried out?
4 List and describe four methods of validation.
5 The secretary of the local swimming club is going to set up a database containing member details. For each of the following fields, suggest a data type and a validation check which could be carried out:
   a) Membership number
   b) Name
   c) Address
   d) Postcode
   e) Date of birth
   f) Gender.

Go online for answers

Online

Data portability

What is data portability?

- Data **portability** is the ability to transfer data from one system or software application to another without having to re-enter the data.
- The format in which data is held will determine whether or not it is portable between different software applications and different computer systems.

Data compression

Data compression is used to reduce the size of a digital file. The compressed version of the file:

- takes less time to upload, download or attach to an email
- takes up less storage space on a computer system.

Software for compressing and decompressing data

Graphic compression can be done using a graphics package. The graphic can be saved using the specified format to a given resolution.

Data files can be compressed by saving them using a particular file format:

- Graphics can be compressed using JPEG or GIF format.
- Music files can be compressed using MP3 format.
- Video files can be compressed using MPEG format.

WinZip software can be used to compress data.

It is possible to compress folders of information and store them as a single file for emailing or transporting. If WinZip is used, they are called ZIP files.

Compressed files must be decompressed before they can be opened or used. The destination computer must contain the data compression software so that the ZIP file can be extracted or unzipped.

 Knowledge of ICT
Components.doc
Microsoft Word Document

 Knowledge of ICT
Components.zip
4,225 KB

Type: Microsoft Word Document
Title: Input Devices
Date Modified: 05/06/2010 10:55
Size: 27.4 MB

This Microsoft Word file is 27.4 MB in size. After it has been compressed, it is 4.2 MB in size.

Revised

The format in which a file is stored determines the portability of the file.

File type	Features
Comma-separated variable (CSV)	● Data fields are separated by commas. ● The field names are entered first. ● Each record in the file is on a new line. ● Files are portable. ● Files can be produced by data-logging equipment.
Rich text format (RTF)	● Scanned documents processed with OCR software are usually saved as RTF documents. ● Files are portable because the file can be opened using a variety of applications. ● Users can transfer RTF data between differing applications: a user of Microsoft Word can save a file to RTF and send it to a user of a different word processor.
JPEG (Joint Photographic Experts Group)	● JPEG graphics are commonly used on web pages. ● This is a compressed file format: files are normally small. ● Files are highly portable: they can be used in any document on a number of different operating systems.
MPEG-3 (MP3)	● This is a compressed file format for sound and audio files. ● It filters out all noise that is not detectable by the human ear. ● Music files are about ten times smaller than the equivalent CD WAV or AIFF files. ● iTunes uses this format for music that is downloaded and for podcasts.
MPEG-4 (MP4)	● This is a compressed file format for video files and DVDs. ● High-quality video can be viewed on portable MP4 players and across the internet.
Graphic Interchange Format (GIF)	● This is a compressed file format. ● GIF files are usually small and are suitable for inclusion on web pages. ● Colour quality can be a problem with GIF.
Text (also called ASCII text – TXT)	● This is a simple text format that holds letters and numbers but not additional information, such as bold or italic. ● ASCII (American Standard Code for Information Interchange) files can be imported into a word processor but the file may not appear in its original format. ● Text files are highly portable and are supported by almost every application.
Musical Instrument Digital Interface (MIDI)	● A sound file format produced when digital musical instruments are connected as input devices to the computer.
Portable Document Format (PDF) GCSE ICT Full Course.pdf	● This is a portable file that can be generated from a variety of file types (for example, Microsoft Word documents). ● The generated file is usually smaller than the original file. ● Adobe Reader (a free download from Adobe's website) is needed to view or print a PDF file but it is available for many types of computer system. ● Generally, PDF files are read only and cannot be edited without special software.
HyperText Markup Language (HTML)	● Web pages are usually designed in HTML format. ● Browsers are programmed to interpret the HTML and to display the contents on screen.

Exam tips

● The CSV file format is a simple example of data portability. It allows data to be imported into a word processor, a database or a spreadsheet.
● The Moving Picture Experts Group produces the MPEG standards for compressed digital video.
● MP3 and MP4 have changed the face of entertainment. Most people now download music electronically onto their computer or MP3 player. MP4 has improved the portability of video.

Check your understanding

Tested

1 What is data portability?
2 Give three reasons why data is compressed.
3 What types of software can compress data?
4 What are the advantages of compressing a folder of data for emailing?
5 What does CSV stand for?
6 What does PDF stand for?
7 What does MIDI stand for?
8 Name three compressed file formats.

Go online for answers

Online

Data networks and their components 1

LANs and WANs

Revised

- A network consists of a set of computers which are linked together.
- A local area network (LAN) is a number of computers linked together on a single site.
- A wide area network (WAN) is a collection of networks connected using a telecommunications link.
- Most WANs make use of the PSTN (see p. 76).
- The internet is a WAN.

The main differences between a LAN and a WAN

Local Area Network (LAN)	Wide Area Network (WAN)
• Spreads over a small geographic area, usually one or two buildings • Can link computers using copper cabling.	• Spreads over a vast geographic area, countries or the world • Is a network of networks • Links networks using fibre optic cable or a wireless link, e.g. satellite.

Advantages of using a LAN

Revised

Most organisations have networked computers rather than stand-alone computers. Networked computers have several advantages:

- Expensive peripherals can be shared between a number of computers. For example, one printer, fax or scanner can be used by several computers in a room or building.
- A single copy of software can stored on the file server and shared by all the computers on the network.
- Users can communicate with each other on the network by email, broadcasting messages or electronic conferencing.
- Users can share files and work on joint projects using shared resources and folders on the network.
- Users have flexible access – they can log on at any computer and access their files.

> **Exam tip**
> You should memorise the main advantages of using a network.

File server

Revised

The **file server** is the main computer on the network:

- It is more powerful than the other computers, with a large amount of RAM and hard disk space.
- It manages file and network security across the network.
- It makes sure that only authorised users log on to the system; the log-in process makes use of usernames and passwords.

A typical server holds:

- network operating system software, such as Microsoft Windows 2007
- application software, such as Microsoft Office
- user files created by the users on the system
- system software, which manages the network resources and security
- utility software, such as a virus checker.

Exam tip

Note that the file server holds more than user data. It holds a lot of other important software which relates to the smooth functioning of the network.

Network interface card   Revised

- Each computer must have a **network interface card** so that it can communicate with devices on the network.
- A network cable inserted into the port on the NIC connects the PC to the file server.
- A wireless network interface card (WNIC) may be installed in a computer; the computer is 'wireless enabled' and can connect to a wireless router, providing mobile access to a network.
- A USB wireless adapter can be added to the computer to enable wireless access to a network.

Check your understanding   Tested

1 Expand the acronyms LAN and WAN.
2 List two differences between a LAN and a WAN.
3 List three advantages of using a network.
4 What is the function of a file server on the network?
5 What is the function of a network card in a computer?

Go online for answers   Online

Data networks and their components 2

A network cable:

- links computers to the network or to each other
- plugs directly into the network card in the computer
- carries data along the cables to and from the file server.

Switches   Revised ☐

A **switch**:

- connects to a group of computers
- connects to the file server
- organises communication between the file server and the computers
- can send data to a particular computer.

Routers   Revised ☐

> **Exam tip**
> Remember that many schools have wireless laptops which allow pupils mobile access to the school network.

A **router**:

- shares a network connection between devices
- enables a LAN to connect to the internet or a WAN and allows the two networks to communicate
- may have integrated security features, such as a **firewall**
- translates information from the internet so that the computers on a LAN can understand it.

A router can be *wired* or *wireless*. A wireless **router** or wireless access point:

- can allow a computer to connect to a LAN
- can enable home users to connect to the internet without the inconvenience of cables.

Computers that connect to a wireless router or wireless access point must contain a wireless network interface card or must be wireless enabled.

Network software   Revised ☐

When a computer is part of a network, network software must be installed on it. This allows it to communicate with the file server and other computers.

The need for communications protocols   Revised ☐

A communications **protocol** is an agreed standard or set of rules for sending or receiving data on a network.

- If a computer receives data on a network, it must support the communications protocol of the sending computer.
- The protocol used on the internet is Transmission Control Protocol/Internet Protocol (TCP/IP).
- TCP/IP makes sure that data is not lost as it travels from one computer to another.

- The protocol used to transmit data around a LAN may be different.
- If your school network is connected to the internet then the computers must be able to understand the TCP/IP protocol.
- The router used to connect two networks (a LAN and the internet) performs a translation function and allows computers of differing protocols to communicate.

Check your understanding   Tested ☐

1 What is the role of a switch on a network?
2 How is a router used on a network?
3 What security feature can be built into a router?
4 How can computers connect to a wireless router?
5 What are communications protocols and why are they needed?

Go online for answers   Online ☐

Digital communication security 1

A network must be secured and protected from threats, including:

- viruses, such as Trojan horses and worms
- unauthorised access by users or **hackers**
- authorised users who might damage important files
- unexpected breakdown resulting in the loss of data
- physical damage.

The measures discussed here help to protect the network.

Usernames and passwords

Each user on the network is given a unique username. The user decides on a **password** which only they will know. It is important to select a *secure* password.

A secure password should:

- be a combination of letters and numbers
- have a minimum number of characters
- be changed regularly
- be kept confidential.

A secure password should not:

- be your username, pet's name or family name
- a word (if you say it, someone can remember it and use it when you are not there)

- be written down anywhere.

The username and password are used when logging on to the computer system. This helps prevent unauthorised users from getting onto the network.

Levels of access

Levels of access are used to limit the things which users can do on the network. In a school, pupils, teachers and the system manager have different levels of access.

A pupil can:	A teacher can do what pupils can and also:	The system manager can do what teachers and pupils can and also:
<ul><li>access software</li><li>use the internet</li><li>change the content and location of their user files</li><li>change their password</li><li>use a printer</li><li>connect and use portable storage devices.</li></ul>	<ul><li>give pupils printer credits</li><li>reset pupils' passwords</li><li>monitor pupils' activity using special software</li><li>set up shared folders for pupils to use.</li></ul>	<ul><li>set up new users</li><li>remove users</li><li>allocate disk storage space to users</li><li>copy files between users</li><li>allocate network resources, such as printers</li><li>connect new devices</li><li>install software, such as printer drivers.</li></ul>

Encryption

- Data can be encrypted to prevent unauthorised access or to keep it secure whilst being transmitted over a network.
- Data is encrypted or encoded using encryption key software.
- Encrypted data is unreadable to anyone who intercepts it.

- Data is decrypted or decoded when it reaches its destination using encryption software.
- Only a user with the encryption key can read the data.
- Data can also be stored in encrypted form.

Measures that prevent information systems from misuse

Revised

An 'information system' includes all the components used for the input, output, storage and processing of data. The entire information system must be protected.

Virus protection

A **virus** is a computer program designed to damage some aspect of an information system. Virus protection software should be installed to prevent virus attacks and should be updated regularly so that new viruses can be identified. It should also perform regular scans of the computer system.

Viruses can enter a network through:

- portable storage devices, such as flash memory sticks
- the internet
- email attachments.

Virus protection software scans the system for threats. If a device contains a virus the user and system administrator will be notified.

Virus protection software can protect against the following kinds of threat:

- worms that spread by replication and do not have to be attached to a document or program; a worm slows down processing on the network while it is reproducing
- Trojan horses that gain entry to a user's computer 'in disguise' – the user may think that it is a useful program; a Trojan horse provides **hackers** with an entry point to the user's computer
- **spam**, which involves bulk sending of electronic messages to people who have not requested the

information; internet users see spam as junk emails which can fill their inbox

- **spyware**, that is, malicious software (malware) which is secretly installed on a user's computer; spyware collects information about the user and can change computer settings or monitor keystrokes so that passwords can be captured; anti-spyware software has now become part of ensuring that a computer system is kept secure.

> **Exam tip**
>
> You need to provide the *full* definition of a virus. There are two parts to it:
> - a computer program
> - designed to damage some aspect of an information system.

> **Exam tip**
>
> Examiners may ask you about worms, Trojan horses, spyware and spam to test your understanding of viruses and virus protection in general.

Firewalls

A **firewall** can be integrated into a hardware device or a software program. It filters information coming from the internet to the computer network.

A firewall can prevent:

- **hackers**, viruses and spam from entering the network via the internet
- users and computers within the network from uploading data to the internet.

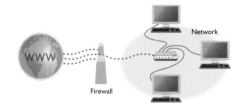

Check your understanding

Tested

1 List four threats which a network faces.
2 How can a username and password be used as a security measure on a network?
3 What are the characteristics of a good password?
4 How do levels of access help provide security on a network? Give an example of differing security levels.
5 What is encryption and how does it protect data on a network?
6 How can virus attacks be avoided on a computer system?
7 List two types of virus and describe how they work.
8 What is the function of a firewall on a network?

Go online for answers

Online

Digital communication security 2

Revised

Backing up data

Most network systems use a **backup** process to make sure that there is a copy of the data that can be loaded on to the system if the original data is lost.

A backup is a copy of the original data. Backing up should be carried out regularly to minimise the amount of data lost if a problem occurs. Data on a network should be backed up daily. PC users should also back up their data regularly.

Backing up data on a LAN

LAN data can be backed up to an external hard disk or magnetic tape.

A hard disk can be attached to a network:

- through a network point (known as a network-attached storage (NAS) device)
- directly to the main computer (known as a direct-attached storage (DAS) device).

When a backup is scheduled, all of the files from the file server are copied onto the hard disk.

A NAS device can share data with other servers and devices on the network but a DAS device cannot.

Backup to magnetic tape has become less popular but has the following characteristics:

- The tape is stored in the tape drive on the file server.
- A backup of the system is taken at regular intervals. Backup activity may slow the network down as it uses system resources.
- Backup is scheduled when the computer system is not busy, for example, during the night.
- Tapes are kept for an agreed period before being reused.

Backing up data on a PC

Most operating systems include a special utility which makes it easy for users to back up data. A wizard may guide users through the process.

A high-capacity external hard drive can be attached to a computer, generally using a USB cable, and files can be backed up to it. A backup can also be made to the existing hard disk or to a removable storage medium, such as CD-R, CD-RW or DVD.

The advantages of using CD or DVD are:

- high capacity
- low cost
- portability.

Using online storage for backup from a LAN or a PC

- Data is uploaded to a location such as a secure server online.
- Backup can be scheduled to be completed automatically.
- Files can be accessed from any computer connected to the network.

A disadvantage is that it may not be acceptable to store sensitive data on the internet.

Check your understanding

Tested

1 What is a 'backup'?
2 Why is the backup of data important in any computer system?
3 List three ways of backing up data on a network.
4 How can data on a PC be backed up?
5 How can storage online be used for backup?
6 What is the advantage of using online storage?

Go online for answers

Online

Mobile digital communication

Mobile communication devices Revised ☐

Wireless technologies use radio waves to transmit data. **Wi-Fi**, **3G** and **Bluetooth** wireless technologies have increased the use of mobile devices. Most mobile devices feature at least two of the three technologies.

Mobile technology provides a high level of flexibility for users. They can communicate, access information, use the internet and talk whilst on the move. Businesses, schools and medicine make use of wireless-enabled devices.

Mobile phones
- use radio frequency to transmit data
- are small, portable and easy to carry around
- can be used anywhere that there is network coverage
- can 'roam' – this means they can send and receive data and telephone calls from anywhere in the world
- can often take digital photographs or short movies
- can send a text message instantly to a mobile phone on any network
- can receive a text message while a call is in progress
- can send emails
- can take a voicemail message if the owner of the telephone is not available.

Smartphones and personal digital assistants (PDAs)
- are hand-held devices that combine internet services and mobile phone functions
- use Wi-Fi and 3G technologies to communicate
- can access the internet and receive full email attachments
- function as a mobile phone
- provide many, if not all, of the functions of a mobile phone.

Blackberry and iPhone products are smartphones or personal digital assistants (PDAs).

Laptops
- are wireless-enabled – they have a wireless adapter fitted
- can be connected to a wireless network using Wi-Fi technology
- use Bluetooth technology to pair with devices which are close, for example, printers.

This table summarises how some devices use wireless technology.

Device	Technology available	Possible uses
Mobile phone	Bluetooth	Connecting to other mobile phones to transfer pictures or MP3 files
	3G and WAP	Connecting to the internet to download webpages in a suitable format
Smartphone or Personal Digital Assistant (PDA)	Bluetooth	Connecting to a hands-free or Bluetooth headset Connecting to another Bluetooth-enabled device to transfer photos or music
	Wi-Fi	Connecting to the internet on the move, for example, connecting to a wireless network in a hotel or airport
	3G	Connecting to the internet when Wi-Fi is not available
Laptop	Wi-Fi	Connecting to a wireless LAN via a router to access the server and all peripherals available to network users
	Bluetooth	Connecting to other Bluetooth-enabled devices, such as printers, other laptops and cameras

Wi-Fi (wireless fidelity)

- Devices connecting to a Wi-Fi network must have a wireless adapter.
- Wi-Fi hotspots are in city centres, hotels and airports.
- Computer users buy a voucher and connect their device to the Wi-Fi network and internet.
- Data can be transmitted at speeds of up to 54 megabits per second (Mbps).
- A wireless router for internet access uses Wi-Fi.
- Secure networks can be set up using Wi-Fi, which has a recognised standard created by IEEE.

Advantages	Disadvantages
- Users can log on in any location. - Users can use a wide range of devices. - A network can be set up without wires. - Prices are decreasing. - Devices can roam from one network to another.	- Signal strength varies according to distance from the wireless router. - The connection may not be as secure as a wired connection. - Interference from other wireless sources may distort data signals. - Weather conditions may affect the connection.

3G (third generation)

- A subscription to a service provider – usually a mobile phone company – is needed.
- Access to the internet is available from any location which has network coverage.
- Tariffs charge with the amount of data downloaded, so it can be expensive.
- International tariffs are particularly expensive.
- Data transfer speeds are slower than Wi-Fi.

Advantages	Disadvantages
- Coverage is available where normal broadband is not. - Devices can also be used for voice calls and a range of other data services. - Video calling is possible. - Map and positioning services are available.	- Performance is affected by network coverage and the strength of the signal. - Increased power consumption requires a larger, high-capacity battery. - Data transfer can be expensive. - High bandwidth (e.g. watching TV) cannot be carried out using 3G. - Download times are affected by the number of users in a network cell and the amount of data being downloaded.

Bluetooth

- Bluetooth is a short-range wireless technology.
- The signal does not travel for a long distance.
- Devices communicating must be relatively close.
- Bluetooth uses less power than other wireless technologies and is much cheaper.

Advantages	Disadvantages
<ul><li>Signal can penetrate solid objects.</li><li>Line of sight is not needed.</li><li>The cost is lower and less power is used than with other technologies.</li><li>Devices are easily connected to other Bluetooth-enabled devices.</li></ul>	<ul><li>Signal carries over only a short range.</li><li>Security is at a lower level.</li><li>Data transmission rate is lower.</li></ul>

Wireless Application Protocol (WAP)

- WAP is a communication protocol.
- Allows hand-held devices access to the internet.
- A WAP-enabled mobile phone uses a micro-browser to display information.

Advantages	Disadvantages
<ul><li>Coverage is available where normal broadband is not.</li><li>Network services and information can be accessed from a mobile device.</li></ul>	<ul><li>Data transfer is slow.</li><li>Availability is limited.</li><li>Graphics are not available on WAP pages.</li><li>WAP is less popular now smartphones provide full browser capability.</li></ul>

Check your understanding

Tested

1. List three ways that a mobile phone can be used for communicating.
2. How do PDAs and smartphones differ from mobile phones?
3. Which mobile technologies are supported by:
   a) laptops
   b) mobile phones
   c) smartphones?
4. Which wireless technology provides the fastest data transfer speed?
5. Gaming headsets can be connected using Bluetooth. What are the disadvantages of connecting in this way?
6. What is 3G and why would a mobile phone user decide to switch it off whilst travelling abroad?
7. What factors can affect download time when using 3G?
8. List three limitations of Wi-Fi.
9. What is the purpose of WAP?
10. Which wireless technology has the shortest range?

Go online for answers

Online

The internet and intranets

The difference between the internet and the World Wide Web (WWW)

The **internet** and the **World Wide Web** are two separate things although each requires the other.

> **Exam tip**
>
> The World Wide Web is an *application* which *runs on* the internet.

Internet	World Wide Web
● Is a network of networks (i.e. all the computers connected together) ● Does not contain information ● Provides transport links for information to pass between computers.	● Is an application that runs on the internet ● Is the largest and most used service on the internet ● Can be described as a multimedia service on the internet.

Features of pages on the World Wide Web

● Webpages are written using the HTML programming language.

● The Uniform Resource Locator (URL) of a webpage usually begins with http://, indicating that the page uses the Hypertext Transfer Protocol.

● HyperText Transfer Protocol (HTTP) sends web pages across the internet.

● Webpages are viewed using a web **browser**.

● Webpages can contain sound, video, animation, graphics and hypertext as well as simple text.

● Hypertext provides the user with clickable links to other pages on the web.

Comparison between an intranet and the internet

● An intranet is a private network website used within an organisation.

● An intranet website uses the same protocol as the web, i.e. TCP/IP.

● The intranet is not accessible by the public – only authorised users can log on and use it.

Firewall security software can protect the intranet from being accessed by unauthorised users. Users use a web browser to view pages on the intranet.

The advantages of having an intranet are:

● Users can communicate using email, bulletin boards and messaging facilities.

● Users can share resources.

● Users can find out general information about the organisation.

● Once the information is uploaded, it can be viewed by everybody within the organisation at any time.

● It can improve communications within an organisation

Some schools have an intranet which is used to communicate with both staff and pupils.

Typical services provided by an ISP

Revised

An **Internet Service Provider (ISP)** sells internet access to companies or individuals. An ISP provides users with a range of services such as:

- a variety of bandwidth options
- an email service
- web servers that connect to search engines on the internet
- website filtering that filters out unsuitable content
- a web-hosting service that allows users to upload their own web pages
- a security package (protection against hacking, viruses, spyware and identity theft)
- software that blocks junk mail and pop-up ads
- online and telephone assistance.

Hardware and software required to access online services

Revised

As well as a PC, an individual user needs:

- an Internet Service Provider (ISP)
- browser software
- a telecommunications line (dialup, ISDN, ADSL), the physical data connection that provides a link to the internet
- a device that allows the computer to communicate with the internet: a modem, an ADSL broadband modem, a cable modem or an ADSL wireless router (depending on the type of telecommunications line).

An ISP provides software that enables the user's PC to communicate with the modem/router and the correct internet file server. It usually comes on a CD-ROM and installs automatically.

An ADSL modem:

- splits the signal into two channels, one for voice and one for data transfer – users can use the telephone and the internet at the same time
- expands the bandwidth available for data transfer
- transfers data from the internet to your computer (downloading)
- transfers data from your computer to the internet (uploading).

It is much faster to download data than to upload data. ISPs make the assumption that most users download more data than they upload.

Check your understanding

Tested

1 Expand the acronym WWW and explain the difference between the WWW and the internet.
2 List three advantages of having an intranet.
3 List four services typically provided by an ISP.
4 What software is required to connect to the internet?
5 What hardware is required to connect to the internet?
6 What is the function of an ADSL modem when connecting to the internet?

Go online for answers

Online

Using a web browser

Revised

Browser software allows users to view and use webpages on the internet.

There is a wide variety of web browsers available:

- Microsoft Internet Explorer
- Mozilla Firefox
- Google Chrome
- Apple Safari
- Opera.

A web browser provides:

- an address bar that allows the user to enter the web address, or URL, of the website they wish to visit.

Address bar

Search field

Navigation bar

Welcome to Maps.co.uk

- a navigation bar that allows the user to navigate between the webpages visited (back and forward) and to reload a webpage using the Refresh button
- a home page that automatically loads when the browser opens; the user can return to this webpage at any time by pressing the Home button
- a list of the user's favourite websites (the URLs are added to a list of Bookmarks or Favourites)
- a search facility:
  - The user enters text into the search field.
  - The browser submits the query to a search engine.
  - The search engine scans the internet for webpages containing the text that the user has entered. Some search engines use a spider or webcrawler that 'crawls' through the web constructing an index of pages.
- a history list:
  - The browser keeps a list of webpages visited in the previous days and weeks.
  - When the user clicks on the History button, the web addresses are displayed.
  - The user can set the number of days that web addresses are stored in the history list.
- settings and internet options:
  - content filtering based on settings provided by a user
  - website blocking based on content and language settings.

Exam tip

It is important to note that a web browser can be used to view HTML pages whether users are online or offline.

- tabs that allow a user to browse a number of webpages in the same browser window
- private browsing, which ensures that the websites visited by the user are not stored in the history list and internet files and cookies are not stored on the computer; this can help the user not to want to leave personal data behind when using a computer in a public place
- customisation options that enable the user to personalise the browser by, for example:
  - adding toolbars, such as the Google Toolbar
  - setting the appearance of the browser
  - managing security settings.

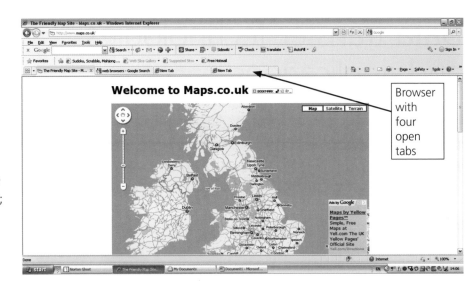

Browser with four open tabs

Some browsers also provide:

- a button that takes the user directly to their email home page
- a button that opens a chat package, such as Messenger
- a button that prints the page being viewed.

The components of a URL

A Uniform Resource Locator (URL) is a website address.

The URL for the CCEA website is http://www.ccea.org.uk. It is made up of:

- the protocol used to exchange information: **http://** (HyperText Transfer Protocol)
- the domain name, comprising
  - the name of the host server: **www**
  - a top-level domain name that is unique on the internet: **ccea.org**
- a country code (in this case, for the United Kingdom): **uk**

Other protocols

- The mailto: protocol enables a user to write an email message to a particular email address.
- The ftp: protocol enables a user to upload webpages to web servers.

Check your understanding

Tested

1 What is the main function of a web browser?
2 What is the function of an address bar in a web browser?
3 Expand the acronym URL.
4 Explain the components of the URL http://www.google.co.uk
5 List four features provided by a typical browser.
6 How can private browsing help people who are using the internet in public places?

Go online for answers

Online

Data transfer technologies and applications

Bandwidth and its impact on internet access

- Bandwidth tells us the rate at which data can be transmitted down the communications line in a given period of time.
- It is measured in the number of bits (binary digits) per second.
- The higher the bandwidth, the quicker data flows along the line.

The advantages of high bandwidth:

- Webpages are loaded more quickly, giving the user a better experience.
- Large multimedia files are downloaded faster.
- Connection to the internet is quicker.

Comparing data transfer technologies

Public Switched Telephone Network (PSTN)

- Uses the traditional telephone system to allow access to WANs and the internet
- Has a low bandwidth 28 kbps (kilobits per second) up to 56kbps
- Is a dial-up connection.

Asymmetric Digital Subscriber Line (ADSL)

ADSL provides high bandwidth, known as **broadband**:

- It transmits digital information at high bandwidth down a copper telephone cable.
- It is permanently 'switched on'; there is no need to dial up the server.
- Telephone or fax messages can be received or made while the user is online.
- It provides high-speed internet access; some companies claim up to 20 Mb per second.
- Generally upload speed is much slower than download speed. This is because users tend to download much more information than they upload.

The Windows network connection status dialogue shows the status of a BT Broadband connection on a wireless network. The speed shown (54 Mbps) is the speed between the computer and the wireless router. The user has received about half as much data as they have sent.

Fibre optic cable

A fibre optic cable is made up of fibres of glass or Perspex that carry signals as pulses of light. Specialised skills are required to join cables together. Fibre optic cables are used to connect telephone substations.

Fibre optic cables are:

- lighter and thinner than copper cabling
- very high bandwidth – data can potentially be transmitted at the speed of light
- immune to interference by radio signals and so more secure
- expensive.

Cable

- Customers must be in an area where a cable network is available.
- Subscribers to a cable TV company can use their connection for internet access.
- Digital TV and phone services can also be provided over cable.

Satellite

Users must buy a satellite dish. A computer connects to the internet and receives and sends information via the satellite dish. Satellite connection is:

- expensive
- useful in rural areas where the telephone system is not up to date and where there is no cable TV.

Revised

Communications technologies let people communicate instantly regardless of where they are in the world. They have changed the way we communicate and our expectations of the speed of reply. New technologies include email, facsimile (fax), Voice over Internet Protocol, video conferencing and instant messaging.

Email
Revised

Electronic mail (**email**) allows users to send messages from a computer across the internet. A typical email address is myfriend@theschool.ac.uk.

Field	Description
To...	The email addresses of the recipients
Cc...	Carbon copy: the email addresses of people receiving a copy of the email
Bcc...	Blind carbon copy: the email addresses of people receiving a copy of the email without any of the other recipients seeing their email addresses
Subject...	A short description of what the email is about
Attachments...	Files (of almost any format) sent with the email

Advantages	Disadvantages
● Flexible – can be sent any time, day or night ● Easily managed – less paper is used and all emails arrive in the inbox ● Fast – delivered instantly to any location in the world and to any number of people ● Inexpensive – compared to telephone calls and faxes ● Filtering – protects users from inappropriate communication ● Attachments – the sender can attach any type of file to the email ● Secure and private – emails can be sent securely and privately unlike faxes and telephone calls.	● Technology – the sender and recipient must have access to the internet. ● User error – a confidential email can be sent to the wrong person if the wrong address is used ● Spam – unwanted emails (electronic junk mail) selling or advertising products can be sent ● Alerts – users are not notified of new emails unless they are logged on to the email system.

Facsimile (fax)
Revised

A **fax** machine is made up of a printer and an optical scanner. Modern machines can scan, print and copy documents as well as perform their fax function.

Advantages	Disadvantages
● Fax machines can transmit drawings and handwritten documents very accurately. ● Most computers allow users to send digital files as faxes. ● PC users with a fax/modem can send electronic documents to fax machines.	● A dedicated fax line is required so that incoming faxes are not interrupted by telephone calls. ● A fax machine is expensive to buy. ● The running costs include toner cartridges for printing, electrical charges and the cost of a telephone call every time a fax is sent. ● If the receiving fax machine is not free to receive the document, it has to be sent again.

Check your understanding
Tested

1 What is bandwidth?   2 How does bandwidth affect internet performance?

3 List three connection types available in order of bandwidth, highest first.

4 What is the function of Bcc and Cc when sending an email?   5 What are the advantages of using email?

6 How does a facsimile machine work and what are the disadvantages of using a facsimile machine?

Go online for answers
Online

Digital communications applications

Voice over Internet Protocol (VoIP)

Revised

VoIP technology allows users to make telephone calls over the internet.

- Users can download VoIP software.
- Calls can be made from PC to phone or from PC to PC.

- VoIP is cheaper than a normal phone call as it uses a broadband connection.

Skype is an example of a company which supports VoIP. Users of Skype can make video calls if they have the correct equipment: a computer, a microphone, a broadband connection and a webcam.

Video conferencing

Revised

Video conferencing uses the internet to transmit pictures and sound between computers. It can be done by a single user on a desktop PC using a webcam or with specialist equipment in a meeting room.

Video conferencing requires the following equipment:

- a video camera or webcam to transmit pictures
- a microphone and sound system to transmit and receive sound

- a screen to view other participants
- a high bandwidth telecommunications line
- video-conferencing software.

Transmitting pictures and sound together requires a communications line with high bandwidth such as broadband or ISDN. Low bandwidth may mean that the images and sounds do not arrive together and the overall quality of the video is poor.

Advantages	Disadvantages
<ul><li>Collaborate with other people without having to leave your desk</li><li>Visual and audio contact makes meetings more realistic</li><li>Full multimedia presentations using the application sharing tool</li><li>Meetings can be set up on demand by connecting up to the videolink</li><li>No travel costs for the company</li><li>No travel time for the employee.</li></ul>	<ul><li>High cost of initial setup</li><li>Specialist training may be required to make use of a purpose-built video conferencing system</li><li>Network performance may be poor when video conferencing is in operation</li><li>High bandwidth is required to ensure good performance.</li></ul>

Instant messaging and bulletin boards

Revised

Instant messaging allows users to use text to communicate instantly with each other. When a user types a message, all of the users logged in can see the message instantly.

Bulletin boards provide text-based messaging but it is not instant or interactive. Users log on to a bulletin board and 'post' a message. It may be a few hours or days before a reply is posted onto the bulletin board.

Internet services

Revised

The internet has evolved and now provides a wide range of services for work and leisure activities. Our lifestyle and the way we work has been transformed through services such as online shopping and banking, social networking and the ability to stream sound and video. These are discussed in the next section.

Check your understanding

Tested

1 Explain how VoIP works.
2 What is video conferencing and how can bandwidth affect it?
3 What equipment is required for video conferencing?
4 How could video conferencing help a company with branches all over the world?
5 How does a bulletin board enable people to communicate?

Go online for answers

Online

Electronic monetary processing

EFT and EFTPOS

Revised

When customers pay for goods in shops or online using credit or debit cards they are involved in electronic processing of monies. Money is transferred electronically from the customer's account to the retailer's account using specialised secure equipment. No cash changes hands. This is called Electronic Funds Transfer (EFT). In a shop when you pay for goods an electronic funds transfer point of sale (EFTPOS) terminal is used at the checkout. It is a computer including a barcode scanner and a **chip and PIN** terminal.

Barcode technology

Revised

A barcode consists of digits encoded as a series of light and dark vertical bars of varying width. A barcode can be read by a hand-held scanner or a laser scanner that uses a laser beam to read and enter the code details automatically.

Each product contains a unique barcode. The information on a typical barcode includes:

- a product code
- a manufacturer code
- a country of origin code
- a check digit.

The first two digits identify the country where the product was made ⟶ 50 01935 01432 3

The last digit is the check digit

The next five digits identify the manufacturer of the product

The next five digits are the product code

Each time a barcode is scanned at an EFTPOS terminal, the following activities occur:

- The barcode scanner reads the barcode on the product.
- The barcode is sent to the computer (containing the stock database) by the EFTPOS terminal.
- The computer uses the barcode to search the stock file looking for a matching product.
- When the product is found, the product price and product description are sent back to the EFTPOS terminal.
- The branch computer updates the stock level for the product to show that one (or more) has been sold.
- The product price and description are displayed at the EFTPOS terminal and printed on a receipt.
- If a scanned barcode cannot be matched with any item in the stock file, an error message is displayed or a beep is heard through the speakers.

Chip and PIN technology

A smart card is a credit or debit card that contains a tiny embedded microchip. It is authenticated automatically using a personal identification number (PIN). When paying for goods and services:

- The card is placed into a chip and PIN terminal.
- The terminal accesses the contents of the chip, prompting the customer to verify the transaction details and enter their four-digit PIN.
- The entered PIN is checked against the PIN stored on the card.
- If the two match, the transaction can be completed, otherwise the transaction is aborted.

Smart cards are also used in mobile phones (SIM card) and in satellite TV receivers, to allow access to subscription television channels.

Microchip

Mybank plc   VISA

4321 4687 3457 3336

Valid 02/01   Exp 02/03 V
MR M FOSTER-SMITH

	Advantages of EFTPOS	**Disadvantages of EFTPOS**
Customer	• There is less chance of theft because no cash is used. • Customers using debit cards can obtain cash at the checkout. • Customers feel they have more personal security if they don't have to carry large amounts of cash. • Exchanging money into other currencies when abroad is not an issue.	• Some people don't have bank accounts or prefer to use cash. • Customers may have to pay a fee for each transaction. • Cards are not practical for buying small items. • Cards are too convenient to use for unplanned or impulse buying, leaving the customer in serious debt. • Customers are anxious about card fraud.
Vendor	• Payment into the shop bank account is guaranteed as long as the transaction is properly authorised. • Money is deposited immediately into the shop bank account. • There is less chance of human error as cash does not have to be counted by the cashier. • There is less paperwork for the shop to process as there are no cheques or cash to pay into their bank. • There are fewer concerns about forged money.	• Shops are charged a fee by the card companies for each transaction, which reduces their profit. • Initial set-up costs are high – the systems are expensive to install. • System failures (partial or whole) can cause major problems. • If the wrong product price has been programmed into the computer, everyone buying it is charged the wrong price.

Automatic teller machines (ATMs)

Banks operate wide area networks of ATMs. They are located at bank branches and in most shopping centres. An ATM allows a customer to gain access to their account 24 hours a day, 7 days a week using chip and PIN technology. The services offered to users include:

- withdrawing cash (with or without a receipt)
- ordering a bank statement
- ordering a new cheque book
- obtaining an account balance
- printing a mini-statement (usually the most recent transactions)
- lodging bank cheques.

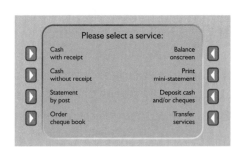

Advantages of ATMs

- Banks need fewer employees behind counters, hence there is a reduction in staff wages.
- Customers have access to their accounts 24 hours a day and 7 days a week.

- Customers cannot withdraw cash from their accounts unless they have sufficient funds.
- Customers do not need to carry large amounts of cash, as ATMs are widely available, hence less theft.
- Using a PIN helps the bank deal with fraud.
- People can use ATMs that don't belong to their own bank, which provides greater access.
- Customers do not have to live close to their bank.

Online banking

Revised

As well as using an ATM, customers can also access their bank account using the bank's secure website. This is known as online banking. It involves the customer logging on to the website in a secure manner using their username and password. The customer may also need to use a bank verification code. The customer may also be asked some personal questions for verification purposes. Customers can:

- view recent transactions
- search for particular transactions
- pay bills online
- transfer money from one account to another
- set up direct debit payments
- send an email to the bank
- view bank statements online.

Advantages for the customer	Advantages for the bank
• Transactions can be done at home, work or on the move using mobile technology like an iPhone. • The website is available 24/7. • Transactions made online can be transferred faster than face-to-face transactions.	• Fewer branches and staff are required as customers do not need to visit the bank as often. • Banks can produce electronic statements, which save on paper and post. • Banks can attract a larger customer base, as customers do not need to live close to the bank

Exam tips

- When learning about barcodes, chip and PIN and ATMs, make sure you can briefly explain how the technology works.
- When learning advantages and disadvantages, make sure you learn them for both the *customer* and the *organisation*. Do not learn more than three of each.
- Be able to refer to applications in your answers. For example barcodes are used in supermarkets to store product information.

Check your understanding

Tested

1 Expand the following: EFT, EFTPOS, ATM.
2 State four pieces of information stored in a typical barcode in a shop.
3 Briefly explain how smart cards use 'chip and PIN' technology.
4 Identify two advantages and two disadvantages of EFTPOS for a customer.
5 List four facilities available at a typical ATM.
6 Describe two advantages to a bank of online banking.

Go online for answers

Online

Billing systems

Applications that make use of utility billing include: electricity, telephone and gas billing systems. Bills are sent to customers and organisations on a monthly or quarterly basis. Producing these bills for a large population at the same time requires a large computer system and uses **batch processing**.

Batch processing

Batch processing involves:

- collecting groups (or batches) of similar data over a period of time
- no processing of data at collection time
- inputting the data into a computer system
- processing the data collectively without human intervention.

Due to the large volume of data, processing takes place at a convenient time (such as at night or at the weekend). During the day, the computer can be used for other activities, such as an enquiry system for customer billing queries.

Electricity billing application

Files used in the batch process

The master file:

- stores information which does not change between bills, such as customer account number, customer name, address details, last meter reading, amount of electricity used over the past number of quarters
- is updated using the transaction file at the end of the batch process ready for the next billing period.

The transaction file:

- stores current data, such as the meter reading
- contains the customer account number (the key field of the master file)
- is sorted into the same order as the master file before updating (to make it easier to match two records with the same key)
- is used to update the master file.

Stages in producing electricity bills

1 Meters are read by meter readers and recorded onto the customer data collection form.
2 Meter readings are placed together into batches.

3 The batches are entered into the computer system.
4 The data is checked, using data verification and data validation techniques. Any errors, such as the wrong number of digits in the customer account number, are notified and an error report is produced.
5 The valid data is then used to create a transaction file.
6 The transaction file is sorted into the same order as the master file using the key field (normally the customer account number).
7 The master file and the transaction file are merged to calculate and print customer bills.
8 The updated master file is saved as a new master file.
9 Customers are sent their bills.

The new master file is used to calculate the bill in the next quarter and the process continues.

> **Exam tip**
>
> Understand the term 'batch processing' and be able to distinguish between a master file and a transaction file in your answer.

Check your understanding

1 State four features of batch processing.
2 Distinguish between a transaction file and a master file.
3 Describe how batch processing is used to produce electricity bills.

Go online for answers

Virtual reality and simulation

A **virtual reality** system enables a person to move through and react within an environment simulated by a computer. The **simulation** is a computer program that models a real-life situation. Simulations and virtual reality are designed with computer-controlled graphics to generate realistic scenes using 3D modelling with which the user can fully interact.

The user is given the impression that they are actually in the situation (the virtual world) created by the computer. This is done using specialised devices to stimulate the user's senses including sight, sound and smell. Devices include:

- stereoscopic helmets (head-mounted devices, HMD) to allow 3D visuals and hearing
- gloves for touch sensations to control the model
- tracking devices (joysticks) for navigation.

Applications of virtual reality and simulation
Revised ☐

Training airline pilots

An aircraft simulator:

- is a full-size replica of a typical cockpit
- shows the layout of runways and the surrounding environment using high-quality graphics
- gives pilots an experience of real environments:
  - ■ flying a plane in turbulence, thunderstorms, snowstorms
  - ■ landing a plane on an icy runway
  - ■ flying a plane with only one engine working
  - ■ dealing with a range of emergencies
  - ■ landing at different airports around the world
- records the pilot's actions for use in providing feedback.

Computer gaming

Computer games are designed with virtual reality. For example, a football game could simulate a World Cup final. Computer games involve the designer programming a set of rules (a model) for the user to follow. The rules define the range of characters, their characteristics and their environment. For example, a Formula One car racing game:

- defines racers, cars and racing circuits based on real-life Formula One
- uses devices that simulate the throttle, the gears and the steering wheel.

The user is given the impression of driving a real car including the visuals, sound effects and the sensation of acceleration and crashing.

3D high-definition TVs help the development of these applications.

Using internet technology, users can now play games against each other remotely. Mobile phones are also used to play games downloaded from the provider network or the internet.

> **Exam tip**
>
> When answering questions on this type of application, use proper technical language such as '3D modelling' or 'using computer graphics to generate'.

Check your understanding
Tested ☐

1 Explain what is meant by a virtual reality system.
2 State three devices use to simulate human senses in virtual reality applications.
3 State three benefits of using a virtual reality and simulation system for training pilots.

Go online for answers
Online ☐

Computer control and data logging

What is computer control? Revised

A computer control system uses **sensors** as input devices, to measure a physical quantity. Examples include:

● light sensors to measure light intensity

● temperature sensors to measure temperature changes

● sound sensors to measure the level of noise.

What is data logging? Revised

Data logging is using sensors to collect data automatically. This involves:

● automatic capture and storage of data, without human intervention

● collection of data at regular time intervals without the need for human supervision

● storing data over a period of time and analysing it by specialised software.

Data logging can happen continuously, 24 hours per day and 7 days per week.

Analogue-to-digital conversion Revised

Since physical quantities such as temperature and light are continuously varying quantities, they are described as **analogue** signals. Computers can only process digital signals. Therefore there needs to be some form of analogue-to-digital conversion.

● An interface called an analogue-to-digital converter (ADC) is used to change analogue data into digital data.

● Analogue data can be described as a varying voltage, whereas the digital signal can be described as a digital or binary pulse.

● An ADC is connected between the sensor and the computer.

Sensor	ADC	Computer
Reads measurement (analogue data)	Converts analogue data to digital data	Reads digital data; responds accordingly

Computer control applications Revised

Computer systems that can monitor their own activity through controlling the outputs according to the inputs are said to have **feedback**. Feedback is an important concept in **computer control** applications.

Home control systems

Computer-controlled devices in your home include a microprocessor (an *embedded computer*). These devices include washing machines, burglar alarms, televisions and DVD players. The embedded computer in each device controls the input and output devices as well as processing inputs received.

> **Exam tips**
>
> ● Make sure you know some of the key ICT terms: sensor, data logging, analogue-to-digital conversion and feedback.
>
> ● Be able to refer to examples of inputs, processes and outputs in home and traffic control applications.

Consider a typical automatic washing machine. The user selects a washing program and switches the machine on.

- The microprocessor carries out a stored sequence of instructions:
  - turning on and off switches for water intake and water outlet
  - controlling the temperature of the water
  - controlling the operation of motors, the water pump and the drum.
- The microprocessor reads sensors including water flow sensors, temperature sensors and door open/close sensors.
- Feedback is an important aspect to help monitor temperature settings and levels of water.

Sensors

Water flow ⟶
Water level ⟶
Temperature ⟶
Door switch ⟶
Panel switches ⟶

Control circuit board

⟶ Water pumps
⟶ Heating elements
⟶ Drum motor

Controlling program stored in ROM

| Input | ⟶ | Process | ⟶ | Output |

Computer systems in traffic control

Computer-controlled traffic systems are mainly employed in large cities where traffic is a problem. They are used in different aspects of traffic control such as traffic lights, car park management and vehicle speeding.

In cities, traffic lights are networked and controlled by a central computer:

- Each set of traffic lights can be programmed to vary in operation throughout the day. For example, the lights can be programmed to remain green on roads into a city for longer periods in the morning. These systems are often called *vehicle actuation systems*.
- Feedback helps the computers to make decisions based on traffic flow.
- Sensors can be placed on roads to detect and count cars over a period of time. This data is then sent back to the main computer, which can send signals back to the lights to amend the timings of the light sequence.
- Sensors built into traffic lights can detect cars starting before the light turns green or driving through red traffic lights.

- Traffic lights can be monitored by the computer, allowing faults to be detected automatically, leading to prompt repairs.

Computer-controlled car park management systems can direct cars around a city to the car parks with available space:

- Sensors are used to log each car on entry to and exit from the car park.
- The system can calculate the number of vehicles entering and leaving a car park and can output the number of empty spaces to large electronic screens.

Computer-controlled speeding systems consist of sensors, which can detect and log car speeds:

- If the speed is over the predefined limit then a digital camera captures the car registration number, speed, location, and the time and date of the incident.
- Using the registration plate, the owner can be detected and a copy of the photo is sent, with a fine.
- The data logged by each camera can also be analysed to produce data about roads where speeding is a problem.

Camera   Sensor

Check your understanding   Tested

1 State three different types of sensor and give an example of their use.
2 Identify two advantages of using a computer for data logging.
3 Briefly explain analogue-to-digital conversion.
4 What is meant by the term 'feedback' in the context of computer-controlled applications?
5 Describe two ways in which computer systems are used to control traffic in a large city.

Go online for answers   Online

Education

ICT in education

Revised

ICT is used to enhance and assist with teaching and learning:

● Multimedia software can create high-quality and well-presented homework, projects and coursework.

● Subject-specific packages, such as Geometry Inventor for mathematics, and online website links contribute to enriching classroom learning.

● Computer-assisted learning (CAL) packages can deliver a topic in a multimedia environment, allowing pupils to learn at their own pace. Assessment tools within these packages can automatically record pupil performance for the teachers to monitor.

● Science and technology courses make use of data-logging equipment including sensors.

● MIDI equipment assists in learning and producing music.

● DVD technology provides interactive films.

● A data projector can project a computer screen on to a large interactive whiteboard.

● Technology can assist pupils with special educational needs:

  ■ A magnifier magnifies text so that sight-impaired pupils can read it.

  ■ An on-screen keyboard gives pupils with low mobility an easier way to 'type'.

  ■ Voice recognition software can be trained to understand the spoken word.

  ■ Braille keyboards and printers can assist blind pupils.

  ■ Concept keyboards and trackerball mouse devices can help those with limited mobility to manipulate hardware and software.

The internet in education

Revised

A school LAN can be linked to a WAN to access the internet:

● Search engines allow pupils to enter keywords and phrases for research purposes.

● Schools use an internet provider that filters content, which is a means of controlling what a pupil can access on the web.

● Pupils and teachers can use email as a means of communicating.

● Video conferencing allows pupils to take part in two-way visual communication.

● Bulletin boards and controlled interactive text-based discussion (similar to chat rooms) can be used to connect to other learning partners.

● E-portfolios allow pupils to create and maintain an electronic collection of projects and personal data.

A Virtual Learning Environment (VLE) is a tool to deliver courses. It allows teachers to access pupil work progress and even tracks their 'attendance' record. The main advantages of VLEs in education are that they:

● provide a central storage area for digital resources

● store shared resources for collaborative teaching and learning

● incorporate multimedia into lessons, which appeals to different learning styles

● allow for learning beyond the classroom with 24/7 access to the VLE

● give access to lessons for absent or ill pupils

● provide personalised learning with lessons tailored to individual pupil requirements

● support the embedding of ICT into subject teaching.

Check your understanding

Tested

1 State four ways in which ICT can be used in education.

2 Describe how ICT can assist with pupils who have special educational needs.

3 Identify three advantages of using the internet in education.

4 State three advantages of using a VLE.

Exam tip

When answering questions on the applications of ICT within education, think of all the ICT experiences you receive in all subjects. Some subjects use special software and hardware.

Go online for answers

Online

Employment

ICT in employment

Information and communication technologies have changed the workplace and the way in which jobs are done. Examples of this in the workplace include:

● car manufacturing – paint spraying in car factories is now carried out by computer-controlled robots.

● warehouse work – stock is moved from one place to another using computer-controlled fork lift trucks.

● office work – applications software packages are used to carry out administration tasks and communications technologies to interact with fellow employees and customers.

The change in technology used has led to changing work patterns for employees and their employers. This includes increased requirements for training in use of software and equipment. New technologies have led to the creation of new jobs including software engineers, database administrators, network managers, web designers and ICT consultants.

Teleworking

Teleworking means using ICT to work from home. With the increase in communication technology this has become more widespread.

Advantages	Disadvantages
● Saves on travel costs and time to and from work for the employee. ● There is no necessity for the employee to live within travelling distance of work. ● The employee has flexible working hours. ● People with disabilities can carry out their jobs in an environment designed for them. ● The employer can employ a more global workforce with cheaper labour costs. ● The employer reduces office costs for rent, heating and lighting. ● Fewer cars on the road help to reduce pollution and traffic congestion.	● Employees may feel isolated because of loss of social interaction and teamwork. ● Employees need an office at home, which may add expense. ● Employees need to be disciplined so as to distinguish between home and work life. ● Employers find it more difficult to monitor employee activity.

Exam tips

● Be able to refer to jobs that are done by computers when referring to changing patterns in employment.

● Teleworking is not 'working from home' but 'using ICT to work from home'. There is a difference!

Check your understanding

1 State three jobs that are now automated but used to be manual jobs.

2 Name three jobs that have been created since the introduction of ICT into the workplace.

3 Describe two advantages and two disadvantages to the employee of teleworking.

Go online for answers

Leisure

Social networking

Websites such as MySpace, Facebook and Twitter allow people to connect with others to share information, such as photos, videos and personal messages. As the popularity of these social sites grows, so do the risks of using them as they store so much personal data.

ICT in music and video

The development of MP3 technology means that more people are using the web to download music:

● MP3 players are physically small in size but large in storage capability.

● MP4 compression standards allow both sound and video to be stored.

● A podcast is a series of digital media files (either audio or video) that are released over time and downloaded over the internet for playback on a mobile device or a personal computer.

MIDI technology allows musical instruments to be connected to a computer:

● Music composed can be recorded as digital signals and saved onto a computer.

● Sound effects can be added after the music has been composed and voice tracks can be integrated with the music.

● The music can be edited easily without having to re-write the whole piece again.

● Sheet music can be generated automatically.

Digital video (DV) is a method of recording movies in digital format onto a digital video tape:

● Movies can be transferred directly onto a PC or Mac for editing and enhancing.

● Movies can be transferred using a USB cable connected to the DV port of the camera or a Firewire cable.

● Video streaming can be used to download a video from the internet. The video plays as soon as the compressed data is received rather than waiting for the download to be completed first.

Digital TV

● More channels are available because of the bandwidth used by digital television.

● An electronic programme guide gives viewers additional information about programs.

● Digital TV signals are not as prone to distortion through interference.

● Viewers can record one channel while watching another one.

● Interactive TV allows the user to play games, perform home shopping and vote in competitions.

Exam tip

In answers to examination questions, use other examples of leisure use that you have personal experience of. For example, you may have watched 3D television.

Check your understanding

1 Describe what is meant by video streaming.

2 State one drawback of using ICT for social networking.

3 Identify three activities available on a TV that make it interactive.

Go online for answers

Globalisation

Globalisation

With the development and growth of communications technology, the world seems to be 'smaller' and more interconnected. We now find it easier to contact people and organisations across the world, day or night. People can now purchase goods from any country, pay for them electronically and receive them without ever having to leave their home.

Exam tip

Be able to identify the advantages of global shopping for the customer and for the company.

The impact of globalisation on shopping

E-commerce is the buying and selling of goods on the World Wide Web. Consumers using the internet for shopping have access to all the major stores 24 hours a day. Some customers are concerned about fraud and prefer not to use this method of shopping.

- When buying products over the internet, money is transferred using electronic funds transfer (EFT).
- Customers enter a card verification code (CVC).
- Funds are transferred from the customer account to the seller's account in seconds via communications links.

Large supermarkets have made it possible to shop for groceries online, book a delivery slot and pay by credit or debit card. Shoppers can access products bought on previous transactions through 'My Favourites'.

Advantages for the consumer
● Shopping can be done from the comfort of your own home 24/7.
● Busy people and those with young children may find it difficult to visit the supermarket.
● Elderly and disabled people can have heavy items delivered without the inconvenience of visiting the store.
● Shoppers have access to a wider variety of stores, giving them a greater choice of items and access to more competitive pricing.
● The stores can be anywhere in the world.

Advantages for the company
● The website is open 24/7.
● Checkout operators are not required.
● The website can be reached from anywhere in the world, so the company has access to a larger customer base.
● A shop can set up an e-commerce site and can trade without the need to rent premises that customers can visit.

The need for security for online shopping

The biggest concern most people have about buying online is security.

- Secure websites use an internet protocol called Secure Socket Layers (SSL) that encrypts data to make it unreadable before it is sent from your computer.
- Secure Electronic Transaction (SET) is a protocol used by Visa and MasterCard to make online purchases much more secure for card users:
  - The company sends the consumer a **digital signature** which confirms the company's identity.
  - When sending account details to pay for goods, customers send a digital signature that allows the bank to confirm the customer's identity.

Check your understanding

1 What is meant by the term 'e-commerce'?
2 State three advantages for the customer of shopping in a global way.
3 State three advantages for the company in providing opportunities to shop in a global way.
4 Describe how a website used for shopping transactions can be made more secure.

Go online for answers

Health and safety

Exam tips

- When learning a health issue, make sure you also learn how it is minimised.
- When asked about ways of minimising a number of health risks, do not repeat your answers. For example, 'taking regular breaks' can be a valid way of minimising a number of health risks, but you only get credit once for using it in your answer.

Health and safety

Revised

As ICT has been fully integrated into the workplace, this has led to an increase in health and safety issues. It is the responsibility of an employer to provide a working environment which addresses these health and safety issues.

Health issues

Revised

Issue	What is the issue?	How can it be minimised?
Repetitive strain injury (RSI)	• A range of conditions affecting the muscles and joints in the neck, shoulders, arms, wrists and hands • Occurs when the same muscle groups perform the same actions over and over again, such as constantly keying data using a keyboard	• Take regular breaks • Use an ergonomically designed keyboard and mouse • Use appropriate furniture, such as an adjustable swivel chair • Use a wrist rest
Eyestrain	• Headaches, blurred vision and a deterioration in eyesight • Caused by overexposure to screens	• Use an anti-glare screen • Use swivel bases on screens to deflect light • Use screens with adjustable brightness and contrast • Have regular eye tests (provided by employer)
Back pain	• Discomfort leading to back pain or immobility • Less work is done • Can be related to the sitting position at the computer	• Take regular breaks • Use an adjustable chair with height adjustment and backrest tilting • Walk around to exercise muscles
Radiation	• Computer VDUs can give out extremely low frequency (ELF) radiation • Illness may occur if the user works for long periods in front of a computer screen	• Take regular breaks • Use a swivel screen to deflect the glare • Use an anti-glare filter • Use a low-emission screen

Safety issues

Revised

A safe workplace means that employees will not be involved in accidents. Some measures employers can take to ensure the safety of their employees include:

- Electricity switches, plugs, sockets and computer equipment should be regularly tested.
- Computer cables and network leads should be safely organised using cable management.
- The temperature in the room should be controllable. High temperatures could make computers overheat or employees uncomfortable, causing a reduction in their work rate.
- Anti-static carpet should be used to avoid the build-up of electrostatic charge.
- Fire extinguishers should be nearby.
- Employees should not eat or drink near computers.
- Employees should be made aware of the company policy on health and safety.

Check your understanding

Tested

1 Describe three different health issues associated with ICT and for each issue state how it can be minimised.

2 State three ways an employer can help make a workplace safer.

Go online for answers

Online

Legal implications of ICT

The government is responsible for creating and updating laws to encourage the appropriate use of computers, digital information and software in today's society.

This law deals with problems involving hacking, viruses and other nuisances by making them illegal.

People involved in digital crimes are known as **hackers**. They intentionally access computer systems without consent or authorisation.

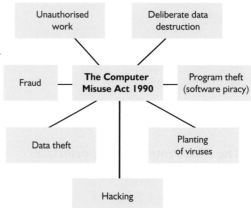

- Hacking can happen remotely through the internet.
- Hacking can involve the 'planting of a virus'.
- A **virus** is a piece of software designed to disrupt the normal operation of a computer.
- A virus can be attached to an email and activated when the email is opened.

Some viruses can destroy user files, others display annoying messages while some store themselves as 'hidden' files on your hard drive to be triggered on a certain date.

Spyware is a program that installs itself on a computer to automatically collect personal user information (such as usernames and passwords used for banking) over a period of time without the user's knowledge or consent.

This law was designed to protect the property rights of people and organisations that create and produce material based on original ideas. These rights are referred to as 'intellectual property'.

The main ICT areas covered by legislation are:

- software piracy, which includes the illegal copying or downloading of software
- 'theft' by one company of the ideas and methods of other ICT companies
- use of ICT (including the internet) to copy or download material such as music, video or text-based files, thus avoiding the price of purchase
- using unlicensed software.

Software licensing

- Organisations that use a computer network must purchase a licence when buying a new software package to cover the number of users.
- They are then legally permitted to distribute the software to the number of users or computers specified in the licence.
- Organisations that distribute the software over their network without a proper licence break the Copyright, Designs and Patents Act.

The storage of personal information on computers in many organisations has implications both for the individual and for the organisations that use the information. There is a need to control what is stored in the interests of protecting individuals and their privacy.

What is personal data?

Personal data is data about an individual which they consider to be private. Individuals accept that their personal data is stored by organisations including:

● health services
● education bodies
● census organisations – birth, death and marriage records
● financial organisations.

If a company collects personal data it must abide by the principles of the Data Protection Act.

The Data Protection Act principles

The eight principles of the Data Protection Act are:

1 Personal data should be processed fairly and lawfully with the consent of the data subject.

2 Personal data should be used for the specified purpose only.

3 Personal data should be adequate and relevant for its intended purpose.

4 Personal data should be accurate and up to date.

5 Personal data should not be kept for longer than necessary.

6 Personal data should be processed in accordance with the rights of the data subject.

7 Personal data should be held securely, with no unauthorised access.

8 Personal data should not be transferred outside the EU.

Key people referred to within the Data Protection Act include:

● **data subject** – the individual who is the subject of the personal data; can prevent processing of their data if it is inaccurate; may receive compensation for loss of their data or unauthorised disclosure

● **Information Commissioner** – responsible for enforcing the Act, promoting good practice from those people responsible for processing personal data and making the general public aware of their rights under the Act

● **data controller** – the person in a company responsible for controlling the way in which personal data is processed.

> ### Exam tips
>
> ● Be able to name all three legal Acts precisely. Dates are not important but the names are.
> ● Learn the key people involved with the Data Protection Act and their roles.

Check your understanding
Tested

1 Read the descriptions in the table and identify what law is being broken.

Law	Description
	Using ICT (including the internet) to copy or download material such as music, video or text-based files, thus avoiding the price of purchase
	Intentionally accessing computer systems without consent or authorisation
	Keeping personal data for reasons other than the specified purpose

2 What is the difference between a data controller and a data subject?

3 Distinguish between a hacker and a virus.

Go online for answers
Online

Environmental implications of ICT

Environmental concerns in using ICT

Revised

The actions of users, organisations and businesses that use ICT all generate carbon emissions and thus cause concerns for the environment. ICT users are encouraged by society to reduce their carbon footprint. Organisations and businesses that use sophisticated ICT systems are not in a position to become 'totally carbon neutral' but the majority are keen to look at ways of reducing their carbon footprint in line with government policy.

Environmental concern	Reducing carbon footprint
Reliance on road transport and air travel	• Arrange meetings using video conferencing • Install computer systems in cars to monitor fuel usage
Power management	• Allow computers to go into hibernate or sleep mode if they are not being used for a period of time • Use screensavers to reduce power consumption • Label each device with specific power-saving instructions
Peripheral usage	• Encourage users to purchase energy-saving devices, such as liquid crystal display (LCD) monitors • Ensure monitors, projectors, peripherals and their mains adaptors are turned off when not in use • Purchase multi-functional devices, such as a printer/scanner/fax (an 'all-in-one' device), which can be more economical in the use of power
Printer usage	• Encourage users to 'think before you print' • Optimise printer controls such as sleep mode, duplex (double-sided printing) and grey-scale • Use print management software to control the number of copies a user can print
Obsolete equipment	• Encourage companies to break down the components and recycle

Legislation covers waste electrical and electronic equipment (WEEE). Users must store, collect, treat, recycle and dispose of WEEE separately from other waste. Users who dispose of WEEE must keep proof that equipment was given to a waste management company and was disposed of in an environmentally sound way.

Exam tip

In answers to examination questions, you must refer to *ICT* environmental implications. For example, you must discuss using ICT print management software to monitor paper usage in a printer. It's not good enough just to talk about the environmental issues around using paper.

Check your understanding

Tested

State three environmental concerns to which ICT contributes. For each concern, explain how it can be managed to reduce the carbon footprint.

Go online for answers

Online